757   Farnsworth   86
        Portrait and figure
        painting

757   Farnsworth   dup
        Portrait and figure
        painting

NOV 18   103
JAN 28   3761
DEC 17   0759
FEB 10 78   0255
FEB 25 78   renew
MAR 11 78
MAR 11 78
MAR 11 78
AUG 30 78   0255
MAR 11 80   0255
                  2579

PORTRAIT AND FIGURE PAINTING

CAT'S CRADLE   Collection of Mrs. Stephen Landon.

PORTRAIT & FIGURE PAINTING

BY JERRY FARNSWORTH

A revised and enlarged edition of LEARNING TO PAINT IN OIL

WATSON-GUPTILL PUBLICATIONS, INC.   New York

757
Portrait painting

To my wife

Estn
986

Second Printing 1964
Third Printing 1968
© MCMLXIII by Watson-Guptill Publications, Inc., New York, New York
ALL RIGHTS RESERVED.
Printed in the U.S.A. by Western Printing and Lithographing Company
Designed by Betty Binns
Library of Congress Catalog Card Number: 63-18773

FOREWORD

THE GULF BETWEEN the thorny country of the creator and the comparatively docile land of the non-creator is wide and unexplored. There are fogs in plenty; few mariners have sailed this gulf successfully; and still fewer are the causeways built for travelers to cross, dry-shod, from one region to the other.

Jerry Farnsworth has achieved a bridge capable of sustaining a friendly profitable traffic. He becomes increasingly articulate concerning the problems of painters, particularly student painters, young and old. He has been able to project the puzzles and uncertainties which are intrinsic in an artist's first approach to his art — he has been able to enter mind and heart of the layman who reads, and leave him with the impression of an eternal conflict never boring, never repetitious; but replete with challenges to excite even a man or a woman who never held a brush and never expects to.

Actually, in perusing this new Farnsworth book, I have been conscious of an emerging philosophy which rises in dignity, substantiated by the facts of long activity and observation, and yet gentle, tolerant and hope-provoking . . .

The problems solved last week, declares the author, *do not guarantee success in dealing with those which now arise.* True enough — and you can emphasize that not only for the arts, but for most of Mankind's specific endeavors!

For the first time also I have found a reward in learning more about the actual mechanics of a painter's life. As commonly presented or viewed, questions of palette, colors, anatomy, highlights, canvas, lost profiles and all the rest — They are matters both dismal and confusing; and the non-painter should thank his stars that he has been spared these annoyances. But in Jerry Farnsworth's new book they become riddles both muscular and stimulating, like stranger personalities encountered for the first time under inspiriting conditions. Farnsworth has the ability to share honestly and fully with his reader: a prime requisite for good writing.

More than that, this accomplished artist and teacher has acquired (or, more likely, owned and owns in his congenital nature) a kind of jaunty humor which shapes thought and phrase in a way to be remembered. He says, *I could never see any point in a limited palette. Who can play the piano with half the keys missing?* He says, *Every painter I know is uneven. Don't be afraid of doing a flop; you are in good company.* And even when you think that he may be going soft in his attitude toward incompetent abstract painters who have garnished the walls of today's galleries before they even learned how to draw, he brings you up short. *One good thing about the modern movement in painting,* Jerry Farnsworth affirms cheerily, *is that it opened the way for new and endless vistas and opportunities for exploration and development; but this includes, unfortunately, the opportunity to make fools of ourselves.*

It is a general belief that Man profits seldom from the mistakes of his predecessors — that, in customary practice, the Elder cannot make the richness of accumulated experience available to beginners. Hence we struggle through a deplorable historic mural of trial and error, error and trial, messing our fresh mistakes over the patterns laid down by those who have quested before. But Farnsworth has gone a long way toward eradicating this perpetual fumbling, at least within the borders of his own profession. If the fledgling painter will but listen, a sound and melodious voice is willing to tell and to instruct within these pages.

And any other reader will be the better for encountering, amid fresh intimacy, an honorable artist who is able to perform that rarity: the explanation, the revelation of craftsmanship, recounted with vigorous inciting charm.

—MacKinlay Kantor.

6

CONTENTS

Foreword by MacKinlay Kantor   5

1   YOUR APPROACH TO PAINTING   11
2   MATERIALS AND EQUIPMENT   21
3   BEGINNING WITH STILL LIFE   35
4   PAINTING THE PORTRAIT HEAD   53
5   PAINTING THE FIGURE   87
6   SO YOU WANT TO BE A PORTRAIT PAINTER   99
7   MORE ABOUT PIGMENTS   107
8   WHAT EVERY YOUNG PAINTER SHOULD KNOW   117
9   CLASSROOM NOTES   125

Index   141

PORTRAIT AND FIGURE PAINTING

CHAPTER ONE

YOUR APPROACH
TO PAINTING

IT HAS BEEN a matter of wonder to me why so many more people are painting today than ever before. All of us, of course, have the urge to create in varying degrees. Some cannot live without a creative outlet, while others use painting as a time filler. Whatever the reason, it is a good sign that more and more people are becoming art conscious and are not just vicarious participants but actual practitioners of painting.

The fact that there are many more retired folks than ever before, and that people are retiring at an earlier age, helps to account for the large number of art enthusiasts.

Young people are studying painting with an eye to making it their life work. If they are serious and have the real desire and drive, there is every reason to believe that they will succeed.

Whether the reader is young or old, the aim of this book is to awaken and develop a genuine interest in painting and to guide him in the right direction in his search for ultimate goals.

So many beginners flounder about without direction, when with a little help, even without class instruction, they might be painting far better pictures and getting and giving far more pleasure from their efforts.

Looking at pictures. The study of the works of good painters, both past and present, is a great help. By absorbing the knowledge thus gained your

VALERIE *It was a treat to paint this girl's long blonde hair, especially in a time when so many young girls have close-cropped hair.*

taste will improve, you will find new eyes and begin to grasp the problems each painter has set himself to solve.

I know from my own experience that my attitude toward many pictures I used to think were great and ones which I could not understand or appreciate has reversed itself as my taste improved. However, there is nothing to equal the practice of painting to give us a more complete understanding and love for good works of art, and to immeasurably increase our pleasure in seeing the world around us.

Thus, it behooves us not to make up our minds too hastily as to what we like or dislike in pictures and be guilty of stating that old saw, "I don't know anything about art but I know what I like." Instead always keep an open mind and try to understand what an artist is trying to communicate, and endeavor to find something in the work that appeals to you.

There is much in modern painting that does not interest me, but there is much that does. I think the modern movements have been a good thing on the whole and to my mind have made a valuable contribution to painting. Even if only a small part survives the test of time, it should bring us a fresh and stimulating approach.

I think a footnote on this subject by the late Homer Saint-Gaudens, former director of the Fine Arts Department at Carnegie Institute, is worth repeating. He wrote:

These many waves of painting that have passed over us in these last two hundred and seventy years are emotionally bewildering to the man on the artistic beach who is picking his way in search of aesthetic sea shells. Patience, as to what it is all about, each and every one of us must make up his mind tentatively, never permanently; for the fascinating thing about art is that it constantly changes. We must beware of those who talk of color, composition, rhythm and form, or before we know it we will be mistaking the bones of art for the spirit of art. All that the best painters may do is to affect us by means of emotional content of their compositions. Picturemakers are not appealing to

EMILY   *A professional model, with a beautiful creamy skin and red underwear, posed for this canvas.*

our minds but to our feelings. The only necessary qualification for an appreciation of painting is a nature sensitive to painting.

Certainly from time to time great art is acceptable to the untrained eye. Yet often the contrary is true. Contemporary art must occasionally frighten placid persons because live art expresses passionate conviction. Maybe this conviction is valid, maybe not. Neither you nor I can tell just now. So we should take what we like in our stride, but not stride too far emotionally or physically.

If you are going to take up painting, even as a hobby, there is no reason why you should not be serious about it. You probably do not intend to exhibit in the big national shows, but there will be many opportunities to show your work in local art groups and art clubs in competition with others of equal ability, and you might turn out to be the best painter there, possibly even win an award and be admired in your community as a person of distinct accomplishments. The most important thing though is the personal pleasure of creation and accomplishment.

Most people, I find, start as "Sunday painters," using their vacations and spare time to pursue this best of all hobbies, if one cares to call it that, to satisfy a compelling desire to achieve something outside themselves and their everyday, routine lives.

There is the classical example of Grandma Moses who started at seventy-five to become one of America's best-known and best-loved painters. Also Sir Winston Churchill, who raised himself well above the amateur class by painting for pure pleasure in spare moments stolen from a crowded life. And many others have been equally successful.

I believe that almost anyone can learn to paint, at least sufficiently well to enable him to produce very acceptable pictures; and often going beyond this. Not only may he amaze himself by his hitherto unsuspected talent but achieve considerable success, both financial and artistic if he has the necessary interest and drive.

YOUNG MAN FROM ARKANSAS   *Note the background treatment and compare with backgrounds in other pictures. Here is an effect of a shadow behind the figure, but it is not a shadow.* (Collection of Walter P. Chrysler, Jr.)

You can't do any of these things *unless you want to very much,* in which case the activity that started out as a pleasant hobby may become the most important thing in your life. There is a deep satisfaction and joy in creating something of your own, be it in painting, music, writing or woodworking.

One does not have to be "inspired," a much overworked word and one which you will never hear a painter use; one only needs to use the knowledge at hand and do the best one can.

It is not going to be all fun either. Painting is hard work, as one soon discovers, and the more you learn the harder it becomes. Each picture is a special problem. The problems solved last week do not guarantee success in dealing with those which now arise.

Pictures have a bad habit of going through discouraging stages, and on this battleground lies many a bleeding corpse. There are periods when the execution fails the original conception. If you give up here you are lost. One learns by experience that a discouraging stage is part of learning most creative arts and one must have the self-discipline to work through it.

The Career Student. Embarking upon a career in art, one must be prepared for a long, hard struggle and some suffering, with no guarantee of success at the end. As a future lawyer, scientist, or doctor, one experiences many years of study, work, and privation, unless one is subsidized, but I prefer students who make it on their own.

There are compensations, however. It is a wonderfully free life, allowing you to do the things you want most to do. Your time is your own to use it as you please.

There are always some compromises, unless you are one of the few painters able to work in your studio and sell pictures to eager clients knocking at your door. But work done for gain, even outside the field of painting, buys time in which to continue a chosen career and must not be scorned.

I am afraid that there are too many students who love *la vie boheme* so

PEGGY PITTS   *This girl is a red headed neighbor of mine.*
The painting is in the collection of MacKinlay Kantor.

well that they want only the romantic part of being an artist without the hard work that an art career entails. They spend half their nights on the town talking and talking about art and sleep till noon or longer next day. Work? What work? My guess is that these unfortunates would never amount to anything anyway; that they are only camp followers who hang upon the fringes of serious artists. I don't want any part of this type.

Happily these are in the minority, and I have only the deepest respect for the dedicated artists and students of whom there are a great number.

Education of an artist. Most painters I know cut their formal education short in their haste to get on with an art career. I know in my own case this was true, but if I had to do it all over again I hope I would not make this mistake. A well-rounded education can be valuable to a painter, and a few extra years can mean much to him later in his career. I wish I knew more of languages, history, and especially art history. These subjects form a logical background for a well-rounded artist.

While the student can gain much of this by himself, it would be better if he could start with a solid background of the cultural arts — it would hasten a student's subsequent career in painting and give it more meaning.

TONI *I painted this portrait of a pupil's wife several years ago at Cape Cod.*

CHAPTER TWO

MATERIALS
AND EQUIPMENT

IN A BOOK OF THIS KIND it seems important to me to list the necessary materials and equipment which, though only bare essentials, will give a student the proper tools with which to begin. One can add a wooden paint box later and some supplementary colors which I have listed.

PAINTS

Don't waste your money on ready-equipped sets of colors. They nearly always contain many useless and fugitive colors and neglect the ones most needed.

The colors listed here are permanent in every way, and there is not one that can be eliminated without great handicap to the artist. Also there is not one which can be produced by mixing other colors.

1. Good sketching easel (described later in this chapter)
2. Wooden stretcher-frame or two, 16 x 20 inches
3. Several pieces of cotton canvas, 18 x 22 inches
4. Palette, 12 x 16 inches
5. Palette-scraping knife
6. Brush water (see later instructions on how to make this)
7. Small bottle or pressure can each of retouching varnish and fixative
8. Mouth blower for fixative and retouching varnish

BENJY   *In this portrait I tried to capture the sensitive quality of an adolescent boy.* (Collection of Mrs. Frederick W. Herman.)

9. Few sticks of charcoal
10. Painting knife
11. Brushes:

1 house painter's sash brush (1 inch)	2 No. 2 bristle
1 No. 8 bristle	1 No. 5 red sable
1 No. 6 bristle	1 No. 3 red sable
2 No. 4 bristle	1 No. 2 red sable

12. Paints:

1 tube (½ lb.) zinc white
1 each (studio tubes).

cadmium yellow pale	burnt sienna
cadmium yellow medium	raw umber
cadmium orange	alizarin crimson
cadmium red light	viridian
cadmium red deep	ultra-marine blue
yellow ochre	cobalt blue
raw sienna	cerulean blue
Venetian red or light red	ivory black

Brands. What brand of color should one buy? You will find the best colors at an artists' supply store rather than the local hardware or paint store, where little-known brands are generally sold.

My choice for students is the *student grade* of a well-known imported brand like Winsor & Newton (London Colors) or Rembrandt (Orpi), or some of the better American brands like Weber. There is no reason for the beginner, or even the advanced student, to buy the finest artists' grade colors. These cost twice as much and, while they are of a little better quality, the difference does not justify the increased expense.

Set of colors. Do not buy a ready-stocked box of colors. There will be many colors that will have to be discarded. Better to select the colors from

THE SPRING HAT *The arms are important elements in the composition of this relaxed pose.*

the suggested list, and, if you feel you must have a box — it is a convenience rather than an essential — buy a good, serviceable one, 12 x 16 inches.

Palette. It has always seemed to me a mistake for a teacher to impose his "personal" palette (list of colors) upon a student — a palette he has arrived at after years of experience and which he is constantly changing. Therefore, my choice for all students, whether they are beginners or not, is the above standard palette, which is as complete as the keyboard of a piano, so that it is possible to mix full range of colors. This palette may be laid out, or "set," in several ways. However, it is important that a beginner get into the habit of putting the colors on the palette in the same order each time so that he can reach for a color automatically, without having to give it extra thought, which is most distracting.

It will be noted in the arrangement pictured here that from zinc white to raw umber we have the warm colors from very light to very dark. On the other side of the white we have three blues, ultra-marine, cobalt, and cerulean (the latter necessary out-of-doors, but not always indoors), along with alizarin crimson, viridian, and black.

Permanent palette. It is not necessary here to go deeply into technical matters such as the chemistry of paints, detailed comparisons of various painting methods, etc., for all of these things are fully covered in several good books, including *The Materials of the Artist and Their Use in Painting* by Doerner; *The Artist's Handbook of Materials and Techniques* by Mayer; *Painting Materials* by Gettens and Stout; and *Techniques of Oil and Tempera Painting* by Taubes. As a matter of fact, the beginner has enough problems on his hands without investigating these considerations. Sooner or later, however, the advanced student will find such books most helpful. The chemistry of paints, in particular, is an absorbing subject and one which can eventually be studied to great advantage.

The important thing for every student at the start is to learn to paint with a palette made up of colors as nearly permanent as possible, avoiding emerald green, mauve, magenta, and similar fugitive colors. There are many who will say that alizarin crimson is a poor color to include on a list which also includes the cadmiums, and I quite agree. Alizarin is a poor color at best because, though reasonably durable, it is not truly permanent — it is also a color for which I have always had an intense dislike. But there are certain times when nothing else would seem to take its place, and, if employed

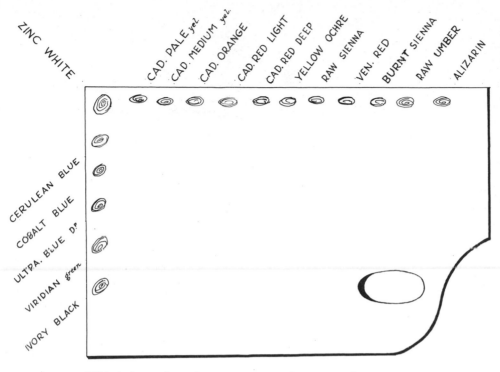

ZINC WHITE — CAD. PALE yel. — CAD. MEDIUM yel. — CAD. ORANGE — CAD. RED LIGHT — CAD. RED DEEP — YELLOW OCHRE — RAW SIENNA — VEN. RED — BURNT SIENNA — RAW UMBER — ALIZARIN

CERULEAN BLUE — COBALT BLUE — ULTRA. BLUE Dp — VIRIDIAN green — IVORY BLACK

This is how the colors are arranged on my palette.

pure or with the blues and black avoiding admixture with the other colors on the palette, it can be used with reasonable safety.

Other colors. There are a number of beautiful colors that can be included in this palette, though it would seem best for a beginner to wait a while before experimenting too much with them.

Oxide of chromium is one of the richest and most durable of the greens, very valuable in painting the head and figure, in admixture, of course, with other colors. It is viridian in its unrefined and opaque state. Although its color is olive green, it is very strong and one needs only a small amount in mixing with other colors.

Mars violet, also an absolutely permanent color — as are all the mars colors — is valuable at times and is a beautiful violet with character and distinction, totally unlike alizarin crimson.

I like Payne's gray in oil, though it is generally thought of as a water-color. It is a cool black, which, when mixed with white, becomes a grayed blue.

There are the manganese blues and greens, which appear under various trade names. These are very strong colors, and permanent, but they should be used with caution because of their terrific staining ability. The blue is like Prussian blue but much more stable. The color fairly approaches emerald green, a green which, because of impermanence, no one should use.

Cobalt violet is a color I have never been able to use. It is permanent, but it seems lacking in character and is a kind of purple I cannot abide. I may grow to like it, however. I have changed my mind about so many things, I may about this.

I have certain favorites, of course, and the student will find that he too will add to his palette colors for which he has developed a fondness and a use.

You can paint a whole picture from top to toe with the earth colors, the colors of the old masters: Venetian red, ochre, and green. Even mud can be beautiful in the right place. Sometimes a beautiful shadow on a face — if you could isolate it and see it by itself — would prove to be mud color. But always set a full palette before you start to paint; you don't leave keys off the piano just because you're not going to use them in a particular composition.

There is, of course, no such thing as absolute permanency, but these colors in any admixture should prove to be about as lasting as any. They should not fade or deteriorate over many hundreds of years if purchased from a reputable paint manufacturer. However, paints are no more permanent than the medium with which they are mixed. A poor medium and an inferior ground can ruin any picture, no matter how permanent the pigments are.

Medium. If you must use medium, a good one is one-third turpentine, one-third varnish, and one-third linseed oil. But don't swim in medium; too much will give your canvas an oilcloth look. Use more paint; do more than merely stain the canvas. Keep it rich, juicy. Load the highlights if you must, but keep the darks flat. Too much medium is the primary cause of paint cracking. Renoir's paintings are still fresh, while Sargent's are badly cracked because he swam in turps, oil and varnish.

Black. If handled properly, black is one of the most beautiful pigments on the palette, but it must be employed with great discrimination. Many students tell me that former teachers would not allow them to use black. Well, of course there is no such thing as a real black in nature; the air between you and your subject prevents you from seeing a true black. But black, judiciously used and mixed to produce distinguished grays, is a valuable addition to

AURELIN *This moody portrait of a young girl is in the collection of the University of Illinois.*

any palette. See what the Dutch masters did with it. One can mix black — or something approaching it — by means of colored pigments, but this seems a roundabout way to arrive at a color that is ready at hand. If the student relies too heavily upon black to darken colors I recommend that he remove it from the palette, at least temporarily.

CANVAS

Cotton canvas is good enough in the beginning. Linen has always been expensive, and it will outlast cotton by many hundreds of years, but that kind of permanence does not concern students.

Whether to use rough or smooth canvas depends upon which produces the best results for you. I happen to prefer a fairly smooth canvas with a good "tooth," as painters call it, single-primed. It is fairly absorbent and does not produce that slick, oily look which I think is unattractive. It took me many years of trial and error to find the most sympathetic surface for my way of working. For the beginner, I recommend a good quality cotton canvas with a medium grain — neither too smooth nor too rough. Find a surface that hasn't a slippery quality but possesses a definite tooth.

Buy your canvas by the piece or by the yard. Figure out a piece that will cut to advantage without waste. Allow approximately two inches over the stretcher size. For instance, for use with a 16 x 20-inch stretcher, cut the canvas 18 x 22 inches.

I have listed a 16 x 20-inch stretcher because I think it is a good size to start with. Don't make the mistake of painting very small pictures; you will develop a small point of view. Make 16 x 20 inches your minimum size.

Preparing your own canvas. When we were students, we used to prepare our own canvases. For very little money we bought light-weight sail cloth or duck. This, in its raw form, could be stretched very taut on a conventional stretcher. Then, by wetting the face of the canvas with water and using a palette knife, we proceeded to work a paste of white lead into the wet surface. The water prevented the oil in the paint (white lead) from penetrating the canvas until it began to dry. If the lead were not applied too heavily, it produced a very good painting surface which would not crack. This method, which I found in the book, *Blocks' Compendium* is used, I believe, to prepare canvas decks on vessels; these take quite a beating from sun and water. Canvas thus prepared will dry in a few days and be ready to work on. There are many other ways to prepare canvas but this is about the simplest and easiest.

Stretchers. With your canvas selected, join the four stretcher strips into a frame — a thing which their cleverly designed corners permit you to do in a moment, making sure that the frame is four square. Next, lay the stretcher frame over the underside of the canvas. You will now see the reason for the extra inch of canvas all around: it can be turned up against the edges of the frame and tacked. Tack the canvas first to the center of the edge of one of the side strips, using a No. 3 carpet tack. (Don't use larger tacks; in driving them you might knock the stretcher frame out of square.) With your fingers, pull the canvas tight and bend it over the edge of the opposite side strip, again tacking it to the center with a single tack. Now turn the frame around and drive a tack into the center of the edge of each of the two remaining strips. With the canvas now held properly in position by these four tacks, gradually work out to the corners, first tacking one side and then the other, pulling the canvas as tight as you can. Space the tacks three or four inches apart. At the corners, fold the canvas over neatly and tack it down. If, on completing the tacking, your canvas is a little floppy, insert the wooden keys which come with every stretcher, using a pair for each corner and tapping them lightly with the hammer until the canvas becomes taut. You are now ready to paint.

Canvas-covered board. The canvas covered board is not the best material to work on, because, unlike canvas, it does not have give and spring. The board is unyielding, a characteristic not conductive to easy handling. Stretched canvas is generally recognized as a more responsive material.

Boards. Beginners often use a one eighth inch thick builder's board (Masonite), in place of canvas, cut to the size required and sized with a coat made up of equal parts alcohol and shellac, which is then given a thin coat of flat white diluted with turpentine. This produces an inexpensive board with a good tooth for the application of paint with the knife, but it is not at all satisfactory for brushes.

While it is hoped that the materials recommended above are sufficiently complete to provide the beginner with the basic essentials, and to avoid wasting money on fancy, often worthless equipment, a few additional items will be described as we go along.

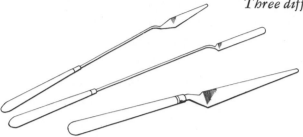

Three different types of painting knives.

LEARNING TO PAINT WITH THE PALETTE KNIFE

Let us now get on with the business of learning to paint. There are so many problems at the outset that I make an effort to eliminate as many as possible. To begin with, there is the problem of tools. Brushes, I find, nearly always confuse the novice. He is inclined to get his paint on too thin. Brush strokes bother him. Keeping his brushes clean is difficult. Therefore, I advise him to substitute for brushes — at least at the start — a good trowel-shaped knife. Many good, practical painting knives serving the purpose very well are now on the market.

With the knife you can mix colors cleanly and easily, and apply them boldly. You will have some difficulty in handling your painting knife at first, but with a little practice you will become fascinated with the possibilities this instrument has to offer. It is a clumsy tool which prevents going into too much detail. It is easily wiped off in order to mix a fresh batch of color. It makes the student see clearly, simply, and in a big way. In short, it is ideal. So, for the time being, we have eliminated the problem of brushes.

LEARNING TO PAINT WITH BRUSHES

The question always arises, "Yes, but when shall I learn to use brushes?" The transition between knife and brushes is perfectly painless and completely unconscious. I have asked many advanced pupils who have studied with me from the outset if they could remember when they started working entirely with brushes. Not one could. It is like a child learning a foreign language — there is no consciousness of the first steps.

Paint primarily with the knife until you begin to get the feel of oil paint and have learned to mix with ease and assurance. Start to use your brushes when you sense that you can achieve the effect you want in a particular section with brush strokes better than you can with a knife. There is no harm in mixing brush and palette knife techniques in the same picture; in fact it adds variety.

How you use your brushes, how to hold them and what kinds of brush strokes to make are things you will learn only through practice and experience. The way you get the paint onto the canvas is of little importance. Better to be clumsy at first and gradually acquire your own technique than to imitate too closely the technique of another. The substance and color of a picture are far more important than technique.

I sometimes lay the paint on in broad strokes, sometimes pat it on in little spots, but more often scumble with a wide brush which does not leave sharp, definite edges. I use the one-inch house painter's sash brush for large areas such as backgrounds, skies, and roughing in. The No. 8 and No. 6 bristle brushes do very well for medium areas, while smaller bristles and red sables are handy for detail.

Cleaning brushes. All brushes should be rinsed in kerosene from time to time, and at the end of a day's painting should be washed in warm water and soap. Rub the brushes on the soap, and scrub with a circular motion on the palm of your hand. After rinsing, shape the wet bristles with the fingers and allow them to dry.

An excellent brush washer can be made with a medium sized tin can (such as a tomato can) with the top cut out, and a small flat can (tuna fish can) with the bottom cut out. With a hammer and nail, punch holes in the top of the tuna can and slip it inside the larger can, as shown in the illustration below.

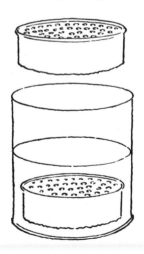

Try making this simple, but efficient brush washer to keep your brushes clean and pliable.

SQUARE-HEADED EASEL
*This is a good easel for
working outdoors.*

Fill the container halfway with kerosene or mineral spirits, which are the best washing mediums, and you have a very efficient brush washer. Turpentine is not the best washing medium. It is apt to injure the bristles, and if it is not washed out very soon with soap and water it will stiffen your brushes. The kerosene or mineral spirits will always stay clean because the washed-out paint from your brushes will settle to the bottom of the can. The whole solution should be dumped out occasionally and fresh kerosene added.

Preparing your canvas for tomorrow. At the end of your day's painting, scrape the canvas lightly; get off the thick paint so that the next morning it will be easier to paint into.

THE EASEL

This is as good a time as any to discuss the equipment necessary for out-of-door painting. Over a period of years we have discovered the nearly ideal easel and a method of holding it down in a fairly strong wind. It is provided with a rack to hold paint box and palette, thus leaving the painter's hands free so that he can concentrate on his subject.

Square-headed easel. The accompanying photograph shows this square-headed easel, which I think was originally copied from a German model. It is made in America by several manufacturers — ANCO makes a very good one — and, if constructed with straight-grained wood and rust-proof hardware, is steady, long lasting, and light in weight. It will hold any canvas from the smallest to one six feet high. There is nothing worse than a poorly designed, badly constructed easel. Buy a good one at the start, and have it for the rest of your life. You won't be sorry.

The triangle. The triangle resting on supports may or may not be my own invention. I have used it so long I don't remember. It is made of three twenty-six inch stretchers joined together at the corners and tacked securely. It can be made of any wood at hand, sawed at a thirty degree angle and joined at the corners with nail or corrugated fasteners to form an equilateral triangle. It's a simple operation, but very handy.

After setting up your easel, place your open paint box on the platform formed by the triangle. Your palette is right before you, the color handy underneath. That's all there is to it. The weight of the box holds the light easel down, steadies the whole thing, and prevents capsizing.

CHAPTER THREE

STILL LIFE   *by Robert Brackman, N.A. This pure still life painting has great solidity and simplicity. This type of subject is directly descended from the great Chardin who was the first painter of simple everyday objects.* (Collection of J. M. Mathes, Inc.)

BEGINNING WITH
STILL LIFE

ALTHOUGH THIS IS PRIMARILY a book on portrait and figure painting, you will find many references to the necessity and importance of painting still life. I believe every portrait painter should spend a good part of his time in the study and painting of this vital subject, achieving a well-rounded painter's point of view towards his work.

A great many students do not care for still life at first, but many come to love it. It is useless to approach a still life as a chore. In the classroom, interest can be stimulated by seeing examples of other students' work who find still life exciting and paint it with vigor and enthusiasm.

The truth of the matter is that painting still life will teach more in a short time than any other subject matter. It helps immeasurably with all the aspects of portrait painting and figure, from achieving beautiful skin tones and painting the costume and accessories, to producing richness, color, texture, and movement. I believe that still life is the purest form of painting, and that for a student there is no better subject matter.

STILL LIFE OBJECTS

It is valuable for a student to set up his own still life subjects, composing them well, though casually, striving to get excitement in the arrangement through violent contrasts and placing the objects in a side light to reveal opportunities for design and pattern in the shaded areas as well as in the objects themselves.

Plain everyday objects are best because they are not beautiful in themselves; you have to bring out what we like to call "homely beauty" in such common objects as pots, pans, old cups, shells, a white pitcher, bottles, odds and ends of things, almost any fruit except oranges and other perfectly round objects. Don't forget that you are doing exercises and not attempting "picture making." With this healthy approach you may, at the same time, paint a good picture; it's been done. Above all, avoid such gift shop staples as candlesticks, cute little figurines, jewel boxes, beads, and the like. Look around your house and you will find a wealth of material. Take a good look at the objects with an artist's eye and your appreciation for the simple, obviously unbeautiful will be greatly enhanced. On Cape Cod some of our students visit the town dump regularly, bringing back many of our best still life objects: an old, broken-down pink chair, broken pitchers, and miscellaneous weather-worn pieces with the patina of age upon them — colors you could never dream up. These have been painted again and again into stunning still lifes.

It's the attitude that counts. There is beauty in nearly everything, if you have the eye to see it — a painter's eye, that is. It is up to the artist to show that from the commonplace, which seems unworthy of the painter's brush, something beautiful can be made.

I remember one time, when I was a student with Charles W. Hawthorne, I brought into class a landscape of the town laundry. It was a tarpaper building with clothes baskets of colorful garments in the foreground and all sorts of faded and bright clothes hanging on the line. It elicited one of my teacher's rare compliments. He said, "I have walked past this place for twenty years and it took a student to point out how very beautiful it is." I never forgot that.

COMPOSITION

Avoid placing your still life objects in a crowded bunch in the center of the canvas; spread them out so that the eye can flow through naturally and easily. Too often the objects are placed on a straight line, which does not allow for interest and depth of perspective. Remember that the space surrounding your subject, whatever it is, is an important factor in the design.

A good still life should, I believe, contain these elements: a rich dark, as in a bottle; a white, as in a pitcher, shell, or dish towel; several subdued colors, such as draperies or foreground color of the table; and one or two rich, bright colors, such as fruit or other small, colorful objects. This should add up to an interesting color scheme which encompasses the full range of color values from dark to light and a full range of color from muted to bright.

Just a slight change in position and perspective can transform a dull still life into something interesting.

The beginner will generally set up a subject of tonal objects without any accents — a close harmony of browns, for instance, with no surprises, no accents of brilliance, no disharmonies, just a mishmash of nothing. Hardly worth doing, I would say. An off-color in a small area, one alien to the general color scheme, will point it up and give it spice and shock. After all, who is to say which colors go together and which do not?

In music we have an analogy: A monotonous harmony is brought to life by a disharmonious accent fitted into the whole. Much more interesting, don't you think?

DRAWING

Anyone, even the most unschooled tyro, should be able to draw simple objects such as bottles and fruit, especially if he is not asked to be too exact

STILL LIFE — BLUE TABLE *by Henry Lee McFee, N.A. The late Henry Lee McFee painted many wonderful still lifes. This painting is a typical example of the simplicity and love he bestowed upon all his pieces. Note especially how well he handled the whites in this canvas.*

in his drawing. He should not worry if the bottle is crooked or the other objects not too precise. By not bothering too much about drawing, the novice is able to focus on the mixing of colors and the handling of his medium.

Ultimately he will, of course, concentrate on drawing, for I believe that the knowledge of drawing can be acquired at the same time one is learning to paint. However, the student should develop the habit of sketching all the time in order to prepare himself for a career in art. He should take a sketch book with him everywhere, on the bus or subway, in restaurants, in the park or just at home. Classroom studies are valuable, especially action sketches from the nude. If you have no model, pose for yourself before a mirror. But at the beginning, forget drawing except for the few following hints.

After you have laid out your palette and have selected your still life objects and set them up in an interesting composition, start drawing on your canvas in charcoal. Try to draw your object in a big way, not a meager little group of objects in the center of the canvas. Fill up the entire area in a bold and exciting manner. You may even let some run off the canvas if you wish; it is intriguing, when looking at a picture, to wonder what goes on outside the frame. If you don't see the entire object, your curiosity is aroused. Rub out your drawing and change it as often as necessary until you have a balanced and satisfying composition. Take your time. That's one of the nice things about still life: it will be there tomorrow just as you left it.

When the charcoal layout drawing finally suits you, fix it by blowing on a small amount of fixative.

MIXING COLORS

With your subject drawn in charcoal you are ready to paint. But first a word about mixing colors. It is almost impossible to tell anyone how to mix colors, although the authors of several treatises on the subject have tried. How can you tell a beginner to take one third of this or that color add a pinch of another and a bit of this or that? I have always felt that one can learn this so much better by experimentation. You can arrive at the color you are seeking in so many different ways, very often without knowing exactly how you did it. Students, I have observed, achieve the most beautiful and harmonious grays without knowing very much about color or without having been taught anything about mixing. Certainly one of the most facinating things about painting is to watch the hue change as various colors are added to it. You

will probably waste a great deal of paint in the beginning, but it is the only way to learn about mixing colors.

If a student is given a formula for producing colors, the results are likely to be quite similar in each painting. Actually, when several students work from the same subject, the results are startlingly different, and each is interesting in its own way.

LOOKING AT STILL LIFE

Instead of painting a solid mass of color and going back later to dress it up with patches of color, start right at the beginning by trying to look at your subject as a jigsaw puzzle, mixing patches of color and fitting them together to form a whole. Disregard the fact, for instance, that an object is a bottle, and study it entirely from the point of view of color, realizing that this particular bottle has no particular beauty in its shape but great beauty in the way in which the various areas of color come together.

START WITH THE DARKS

Concentrate first on one of the large darks, like the blackish-green shadow side of the bottle. Mix your colors, as nearly as you can, to the color you see. Now pick out another dark on another object. With your darks well noted, pick a light patch on another object. Now a highly colored piece. Skip around, not completing any one area, but getting the whole color scheme in your eye. Begin to feel the impact of the whole picture, in this way gradually covering the canvas.

I believe a painting knife is the best tool for these exercises, because in the beginning brushes are too confusing for the beginner. You have to own quite a few brushes, and it is difficult to get enough paint on your canvas with them. Just one tool, a painting knife, which is easily cleaned, should serve you very well at this point.

Do not try for too much finesse — a painting knife will see to that, but primarily try to make your canvas vital and exciting in color. In this way, you will very rapidly gain knowledge in the use of your materials, and your eye will soon become more sensitive. If you go about painting in this manner,

MANDOLIN AND OLD MUSIC   *An attempt to create an interesting composition with two related objects (the mandolin and music) and two unrelated objects (the pitcher and bird nest). The lines in the background are colored silk threads.*

DIAMOND PETAL FLOWERS   *by Henry Strater. Flowers are among
the most difficult of all still life objects; this painting captures
the delicacy and varied color range of a complex bouquet.*

even your second attempt will far exceed the first. Also, you will find that each canvas can be carried a bit further than the previous one. Do not work beyond your knowledge at the moment, but stop when you do not know what to do to improve the study.

VARNISH

If, after the first day's painting, dry spots appear on your canvas, the original richness and depth of color can be restored by blowing on a small amount of retouching varnish. It is worth repeating that you must be extra careful not to use too much varnish. Contrary to prevalent belief, varnish does *not* soften the paint, and it is not necessary to wait until the varnish is completely dry before continuing work on your picture.

There are several good brands of retouching varnish on the market; the imported Vibert, made in France, has always been excellent. Other good varnishes are Rembrandt Retouching, Winsor & Newton, Weber's "Sphinx" and Taubes Retouching Varnish. A varnish should be pale and thin enough to use in an atomizer.

Most students seem to prefer the convenience and ease of varnish in "push-button" pressure cans over the old mouth atomizer type. Grumbacher makes a satisfactory varnish in convenient pressure cans. Damar varnishes seem to be the best for this purpose.

MEDIUMS

I have said nothing about mixing mediums because it is better to use the paints just as they come off the palette. The consistency should be soft enough so that the colors flow easily without the admixture of any medium. This is important at the beginning. There is no harm in using a little turpentine for the preliminary drawing-in with a brush if you are so sure of yourself that you no longer need to sketch in with charcoal. The student should realize that mediums, wrongly used, are a major cause of picture deterioration, often resulting in checking and cracking. Ultimately he will want to learn not only about the various mediums, but about various ways of underpainting, glazing, and employing mixed techniques. As he advances, he can gradually experiment with various methods until he discovers which will be most sympathetic to his way of seeing things and will produce the results for which he is striving.

STEP 1 ARRANGING THE SUBJECT *This photograph was taken after several arrangements of the selected subject matter had been made. Experiment with each composition.*

44

STEP 2 CHARCOAL SKETCH
ON CANVAS *In blocking
out a still life subject, you
can feel free to readjust sizes
and shapes at will. Spray the
drawing with a fixatif before
painting*

STEP 3 THE PAINTING
BEGINS   *This shows how to
hold the painting knife,
using an edge of the blade.
As you start to paint, skip
around in order to develop
the whole color scheme.*

46

STEP 4 JIGSAW WORK *Using your palette knife to cut around an object. Lay your paint in each area as you would a piece in a jigsaw puzzle.*

47

STEP 5 THE PICTURE TAKES
FORM *As you gradually
cover the canvas, you will
begin to feel the impact of
the entire picture. Keep it
always vital and exciting
in color.*

48

STEP 6 NEARING
COMPLETION *Your palette
knife can serve you from beginning to end. Though each
spot will be of a different
shape and color, you must
preserve the big patterns of
color and light and dark.*

49

STEP 7 FINISHING TOUCHES
Step-by-step, you will grad-
ually reach the final stage
with all objects well separated
in color and pattern. Do not
try for too much finish, but
carefully relate each area
to the whole.

THE COMPLETED PAINTING
With the judicious use of color, and without exaggerating its intensity, you can achieve a painter-like study of even a simple arrangement. Note here the definite pattern of each patch of color as it falls against another patch, even in the complicated transparency of the glass bottle and bowl. All painted with a knife.

CHAPTER FOUR

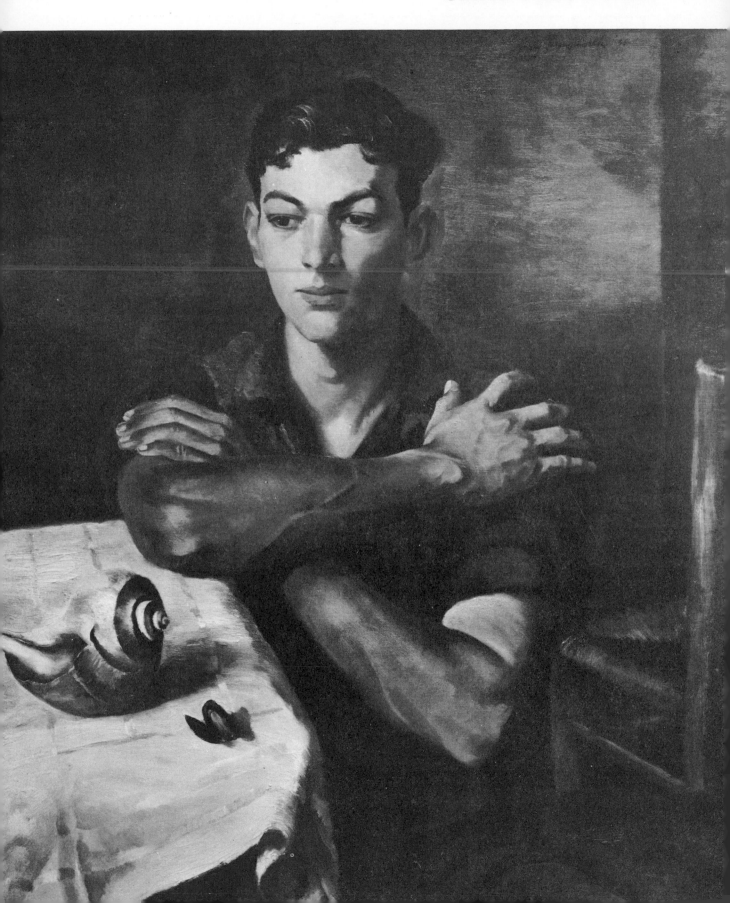

PAINTING THE PORTRAIT HEAD

BEFORE ATTEMPTING TO PAINT the head, the student should have considerable knowledge of basic drawing and how the bony structure and muscular forms go to make up a portrait. But you would be surprised how many, without any knowledge of drawing, will attempt to paint a head, not from a lost profile (I will have more to say about this later), but always from the most difficult pose, such as a head-on view of a model. I always suggest that a beginner, who must start somewhere, stick to drawing for awhile; otherwise he wastes time by taking on too many problems at once.

PRELIMINARY STEPS

The novice believes, since he has not been told otherwise, that to draw a head he must start with the features. This approach always leads to disaster, false moves and discouragement. It is, to use an old cliché, putting the cart before the horse. The very last things to be considered are the features. They are, I have always felt, the decorations on the face. Believe me, you will paint a far better head if you will consider the features at the finish.

You probably know the old teaching ways of years ago. When starting a portrait the teacher insisted upon a very careful charcoal drawing, tickling up every detail, before starting to paint. This, to me, is a waste of time, except

ANTHONY   *is a young Italian boy who was our gardener for a while.*

perhaps for the drawing practice. In the process of painting, the drawing underneath will only be covered up. Fearing loss of the drawing, the student would stain the canvas, using oil as watercolor, so that the drawing would come through and not be irrevocably lost. I won't say that a head can't be painted in this fashion, but the end result looks like what it is, a colored drawing. Since oil paint is an opaque medium it should be handled in a rich fat manner, loading the brush with plenty of pigment.

Composition. Placing the head on the canvas is all important. Regardless of what size canvas you have chosen, the head and body must feel right in the allotted space. I wish I could give you some rules about this, but formuli are useless. I believe that only with practice and an eye sensitive to balance and distribution of areas will one achieve a well-ordered composition. I will say this, however, that it always disturbs me to see a head so carelessly placed that some of the top is chopped off; or a figure placed so low on the canvas that it seems to be dropping out of the bottom; or the head placed too far to the right or left leaving empty canvas that should be filled satisfyingly.

With practice, and it doesn't take too long, a student instinctively learns to fill his composition and achieve a well coordinated arrangement that is pleasing and will result in a fine portrait.

One of the things that almost always plagues the new student is his inability to get the head the right size. I find that generally the head is drawn too large. The student will, more often than not, show me a head anywhere from nine inches to fourteen inches high. When you have only the charcoal outline on your canvas the size is very deceptive; a head has a tendency to grow as you paint into it. Therefore, one should allow about one quarter inch under normal size to compensate for this growth. Nothing disturbs me more than a colossal head. It is abnormal and suggests a giant rather than a normal being. I am speaking, of course, of easel pictures as opposed to mural painting. In mural painting the heads and figures are purposely enlarged for carrying quality. The solution is arrived at very easily by carrying a twelve inch ruler in your paint box. It just so happens that my hand stretch from the tip of the little finger to the tip of the thumb is eight and one half inches. The average size head of an adult from the bottom of the chin to the top of the skull, exclusive of the hair, is roughly eight and one-half to eight and three-quarter inches.

Placing the features. Now we come to the importance of the axis lines.

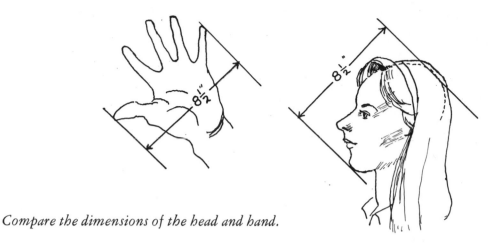

Compare the dimensions of the head and hand.

Bear in mind that the head, no matter in what position, is an oval. To simplify matters we will use only three axis lines (See accompanying diagrams). One down the center of the face shows whether the face is straight forward, turned towards you, or turned away from you. The other two lines show the inclination of the head, whether it is tilted back, looking down or straight ahead. These lines that determine the placing of the features are elementary — and very important. It is surprising how often they are disregarded. They not only indicate the top of the eyebrow and the bottom of the nose, they give a guide for the placing of the ear as well. In normal heads this is between the top of the eyebrow and the bottom of the nose. Do not underestimate the importance of placing the ear. It is a determining factor in the proper drawing of the head. I have seen, in an otherwise acceptable head, the ear placed way down on the skull or high up on the skull. These simple axis lines will aid anyone in avoiding such misplacements.

Crooked axis lines result in the eyes going one way and the mouth another, and sometimes in the nose going in a third direction. Another common error is the inability to observe the necessary amount of skull. The diagram shows what happens when sufficient skull is lacking, the eyes are placed too high on the head and the skull is square on top as though sliced off. The eyes of an adult are about half way down the face. In the very young they are about three-quarters down from the top of the skull. As one grows older the relationship changes, the lower part of the face actually lengthening.

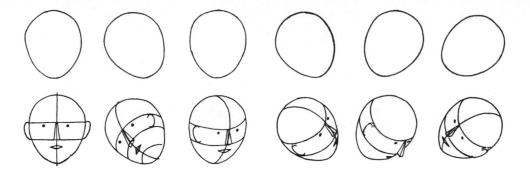

Visualize the head as an egg with vertical and horizontal axes.

Here again no rules, because there are always exceptions and you should study your subject carefully in order to establish these important relationships at the beginning. A hand mirror is useful in studying and correcting drawings. Hold it so that you can see both your painting and the model. When seen in reverse, errors may be far more conspicuous.

So a reasonable beginning should not require too much time spent on drawing, but a gradual improvement and refinement as you continue to work on your portrait.

The shadows. The next step, after you have blown a small amount of fixative onto your charcoal to prevent its getting mixed up in your colors, is to consider your shadows. What is a shadow? The simplest definition of a shadow

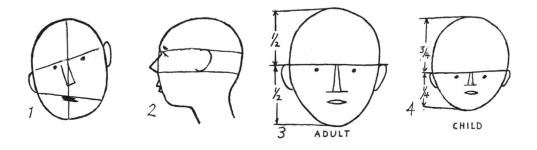

Be sure the axes are kept straight and that you allow sufficient skull.

is that portion of the face which casts a dark, such as nose, cheek, jaw or ear. This would seem simple enough to understand but it always amazes me to find dark shadows appearing out of nowhere, especially in the passages of light where no shadow could possibly exist. When a portion of a slightly darker area is found in the light areas which could not possibly be cast by anything, we choose to call it a half-light. I will have more to say about these areas later on, but it is too soon to consider them at this point.

PAINTING THE LOST PROFILE

In order to encourage the novice to conceive of a head as a piece of color, as in a still life, it is a good idea to have him paint it more or less from the back, taking in only part of the cheek and possibly a piece of the nose. This avoids the disturbing problem of the features, which seems to be the greatest stumbling block for the beginner. This forces him to concentrate almost entirely on the large pattern of dark and light and to be conscious of the great contrast between the skin in light and in shadow.

Lost profiles seem easy at first, but the detail must be very well done to carry. All the little things that appear here in the light are very important, and the ear, in this position of the head, is the most important of all. This is a good way, though, to start learning to paint heads. Features are so concealed that they become unimportant.

Naturally, the student cannot continue to avoid the features forever, but if he does several of these featureless, lost profiles, he will be ready to change position until he sees a little more of the nose, mouth, and eyes — almost a profile. As every painter knows, a profile is a comparatively easy view of the sitter; he has only one eye, half a mouth and a clear-cut nose.

Many teachers do not approve of this "creeping" approach to the head, but I have found that it helps students overcome the mental hazard which the painting of the head presents. *It is a mental hazard.* There is something about the fact that he is painting a person that seems to throw him off balance and confuse him, even though he can paint any other subject very well.

The model should be placed in a good light, with a nice distribution of light and shade. The first things to conceive are the large areas of skin in shadow and light. This is the basic structure of the color notes. A beginner will often pose a model in full light without a shadow. This does not offer the best problem and should be avoided, at least in the beginning.

MODEL RESTING   *An interesting example of the lost profile*
viewpoint in painting the head.

58

If you have blocked in the areas of dark and light, disregarding the features, letting the shadow form the nose and jaw line, you are ready to begin modeling within the darks and lights. At this point try to think as a sculptor would. He has a lump of clay before him and knows that he must form the planes and angles on the face before considering the eyes and mouth. He knows they are in there somewhere, but without the modeling he does not as yet know exactly where.

The Half-Lights. We now come to what, for want of a better term, we call the half-lights. These are the areas that seem to be slightly darker than the lights but are not, under any circumstances, a shadow. These areas are at a slightly different angle from the parts in full light and therefore do not catch full impact of the light. They are generally retreating planes, and, although they are important, they are not nearly as important as one might think. Since they are mostly in the light, they definitely belong to the light side and must never, under any circumstances, be related to the shadows. The lights on the dark side, where a passage appears to be lighter than the over-all dark, we call half-darks or reflected lights.

It is just as dangerous to overdo a half-dark as it is a half-light. Just remember to relate the half-lights to the light side and keep the reflected light well within the shadow.

Paint the shadows in the simplest way, holding the varied tones within the shadow close together. It is a mistake to load the paint in the dark sections of the picture. The lumps of pigment catch the light and cause the shadow to look much lighter in key than it actually is. Keep them flat.

Reflected lights within the shadow should be held down and not be painted nearly as light as they appear on the subject. A too-strong reflected light will tear your shadow to pieces and confuse the eye. Squint at the reflected light and see how it disappears into the shadow.

Often, as on the back of the head, a reflected light appears. This is caused by something outside your picture. There is no reason for putting it in the painting because its source is unexplained and its presence destroys much of the simplicity of the shadow.

When a reflected light appears on the jawline it can be useful in bringing out the drawing of the jaw as long as it is not painted out of proportion to its importance. Students sometimes paint a reflected light as high in key as anything on the light side. Common sense should tell them that such a condition is impossible.

To sum up this important part of painting, remember these simple truths: the lights and half-lights are always held close together; the darks and half-darks (reflected lights) are always held together. If you will do this you are bound to attain contrast and simplicity.

MODELING

After the large areas of light and dark of the skin and hair have been established, you are ready to begin modeling the bony and muscular areas.

Begin with the forehead. See how little variety there is in the light side. Often the variety is a change of color and not a change of value. What appears to be a darkening of the forehead as it turns is in reality only a slight change in color and a softening of line.

MUSCLES AND BONES

Work down the face, modeling the brow and the eye socket. Paint the skin directly over the area where the eyes will be placed, without as yet considering the eye itself; then the simple shadow alongside the nose. Then paint the muscular construction around the mouth, still resisting the temptation of actually painting in the red of the mouth.

NOSE

I have discovered that it helps to look at the nose across the face instead of up and down, as one is apt to do. Also consider the nose as part of the skin of the cheeks pulled out away from the face. It belongs to the cheeks and should be painted as related to the areas on either side of it.

The nose on the light side often disappears into the cheek. No line or tone is evident and it is exactly the same color as the cheek — so paint it that way. It will stay on the face and not become too much of a nose, a separate, detached feature.

EYES

With the face well modeled, all the half-lights well held in light, the darks well established, and the pieces fitted together like a jigsaw puzzle, your head, even without features, should now very much suggest the model.

*When you paint the head, observe the directions
of the light falling on the features and the
distribution of lights, half-lights and darks.*

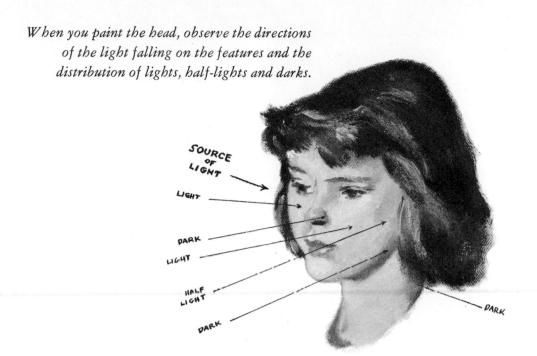

SOURCE OF LIGHT

LIGHT

DARK

LIGHT

HALF LIGHT

DARK

DARK

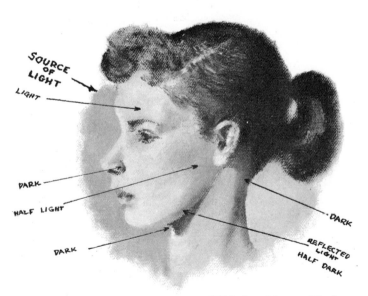

SOURCE OF LIGHT

LIGHT

DARK

HALF LIGHT

DARK

DARK

REFLECTED LIGHT

HALF DARK

*This head in profile has a similar distribution of
lights, half-lights and darks, plus reflected light
along the jaw.*

61

NUDE *by Alexander Brook, N.A. One of the outstanding portrait painters of our time, Alexander Brook has also painted nudes of great subtlety, yet great strength.*

The skin tones should be this model's skin. The skin should be related to this model's hair; this is a valuable part of the subsequent likeness. This relationship is too often slighted by people who call themselves portrait painters, and it certainly separates the distinguished painter from the ordinary one. There is no formula for mixing these skin tones, every model differs and every relationship between skin and hair is different. So strive for the exact color of the skin in light and dark, a near-enough color won't do.

You often see a friend coming towards you down the street and you recognize him at a distance, long before you can see his features. This recognition comes from his coloring and silhouette, whether you realize it or not.

This is important, because no amount of attention to features is going to resemble the model later unless at this point you can visualize the features as they will be when you have painted them in.

You should now be able to see just where the features should go. In the logical procedure for modeling the head, you are now ready for the decorations on the face.

Match the color of the iris of the eyes and paint both in at the same time. Be sure to note the axis at which they are set in the eye socket. Now locate the dark line of the lash and the modeling of the fold of the upper lid above it. Next, the whites of the eyes, noting how far below white in value they are. Generally two lighter whites and two darker will appear in the eyes. Almost always one white in the eye will catch more light than the others, making it the lightest. Note this and establish it. Note the size and exact location of the pupil next. A misplaced pupil will look like a damaged eye, and both pupils are the same size. Place the highlight where it belongs, just beneath the eye lash, generally very near the pupil. Some painters leave out the highlight altogether — I often do myself. The glassy look that highlights give is unpleasant and tends to destroy any illusion of mystery which the eyes might otherwise have. The common error is to make the highlights too big and too white; a heavy highlight gives the eye a blind look; a too-white pupil will give a glassy appearance. Look at the highlight carefully and note that it is not pure white and that it is a small dot located off to one side of the pupil. Even if it appears to be in the center of the pupil, don't paint it there. It is just a trick of light and is better moved over between the pupil and iris.

STEP 1
One way to paint the eye is to place the iris in relationship to the nose and brow, noting the color of the iris, but without the pupil or lash as yet.

STEP 2
Add the lash, the whites of the eye and the tear duct.

STEP 3
Add the pupil and the fold of skin over the eye.

STEP 4
Here is the complete eye, with modeling above and below and the highlight added.

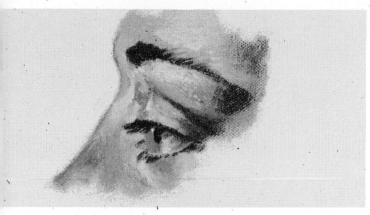

The eye in full profile. At this angle, one sees only a tiny disk of the iris with the pupil set deeply within it.

In this view one sees a little more of the eye. The whites of the eye are also visible.

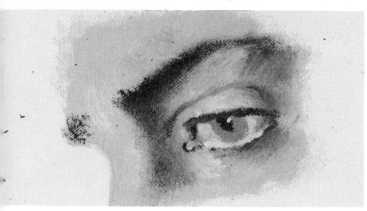

The head lowered shows more of the eyelid and the skin form below the iris.

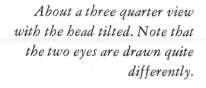

About a three quarter view with the head tilted. Note that the two eyes are drawn quite differently.

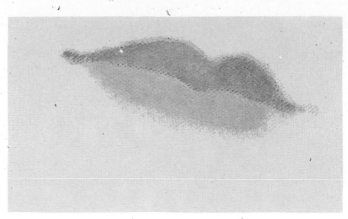

STEP 1
*When you paint the mouth,
first tentatively place the upper
and lower lips.*

STEP 2
*Paint the difference in color
between the upper and lower
lips.*

STEP 3
*Add a little more modeling
of the lips.*

STEP 4
*The complete mouth shows
additional modeling and an
accented line between the
upper and lower lips.*

The mouth as seen when the head is tilted slightly back and turned. Note the form between the upper and lower lips.

The mouth in profile. In this view one sees only half a mouth. The upper and lower lips are quite different in both color and form.

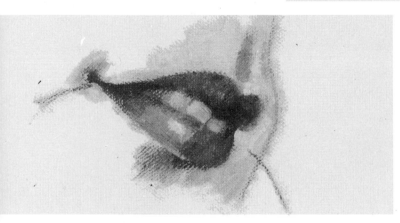

The mouth in a three quarter view and slightly tilted, with a smile. It is very difficult to paint a mouth with the teeth showing.

An almost straight-on view with the lips closed. The upper lip is usually much darker than the lower.

MY FRIEND STEPHEN   *In this portrait, the blurred
shapes of the background have been composed to
dramatize the head, underplaying the pattern of the shirt.*

There is, of course, much more to painting the eye than this. A student should paint into the eye everything he can find there, the construction of the tear duct, the under lid and lash. If the paint gets too hard and fast, scrape it and go into it once more.

MOUTH

The mouth is not as difficult as the eyes, notwithstanding the legend that most of the expression and likeness is centered there. It should be painted simply, noting the difference in color between the upper and lower lip. A great deal of the character lies in the drawing, shape and color of the center line which separates the upper and lower lips.

Try to look at the whole head while painting the mouth. If you concentrate on the mouth alone, you may make it too hard and possibly too dark.

COSMETICS

The question of cosmetics is a tough one. The purpose of cosmetics is to conceal blemishes, to enhance the coloring, and to bring out the good points of the face. Often it does just the opposite. Pancake make-up, for instance, covers up the semi-transparency and translucent quality of the skin. No make-up can improve the skin that Nature gave us.

The same is true with lipstick. There is no red on the face any redder than Venetian red (light red), unless the sitter has applied lipstick, in which case it is necessary to use the two cadmiums, light and dark. It is unfortunate that you have to paint lipstick in a portrait, because it usually makes the mouth too important and too red, even if well applied. However, you can handle it with a certain softness, trying to avoid making it look as though you could slip your fingernail under the edge and peel it off. Paint it on your picture better than the model has applied it herself, improving the color and relating it to the skin and disregarding the shade of lipstick (which may be fashionable at the moment). She will probably try to buy your color next week and apply it with more skill.

EAR

Never does a painter more thoroughly disclose the absence or presence of painting know-how than when he paints an ear. The ear should be well drawn and painted in two or three tones and never slighted, as it often is.

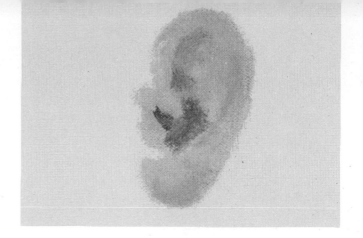

STEP 1
Paint the two essential tones first: The all over light tones and the patches of dark.

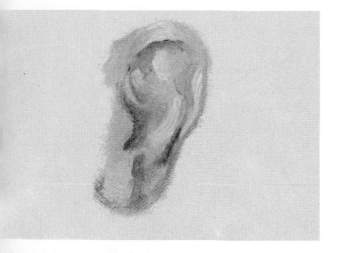

STEP 2
Then show the dark convolutions at the outer rim and the center darks.

STEP 3
Develop the form further, with the addition of highlights.

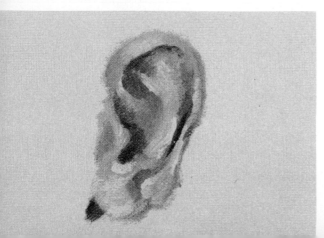

STEP 4
The ear is finished with special attention to the forms which go to make up the completed ear.

The ear in direct profile. In this view, the most complete view possible, the ear lies flat against the head and the modeling is easy to see.

The ear as it appears in almost full face.

This is the ear seen a little less than full profile.

This is the way the ear appears in a lost profile, that is, with the head turned slightly away. Note how the ear stands away from the head.

The ear is placed, as everyone should know, between the axis line drawn from the top of the eyebrow and another line from the bottom of the nose, except in rare cases where the model has unusually large or small ears.

Note the angle at which the ear is joined onto the head. In a profile, look at the slope of the nose and then the relationship between this and the angle of the ear. (See accompanying illustration.)

It is very rewarding to spend plenty of time improving the quality of the painting and drawing of the ear. Never throw it out of focus, as a camera would do, in an effort to lose its edges, but paint what you see, noting the difference in color between it and the rest of the features.

FEATURE RELATIONSHIP AND HIGHLIGHTS

So often in a profile the relationship of the features is not noted carefully enough. You have only to draw an imaginary line down from the brow to find how much of the face lies before the line or behind it.

Keep highlights in a portrait subdued. Nothing is worse than highlights flashing all over the face. A common fault is to make the highlights too chalky. If, on a warm skin, they appear to be bluish, they actually are not, even though they are undoubtedly cooler than the rest of the skin. If the skin is a warm ochre color, the effect of coolness can be achieved by painting the highlight towards the pink without the addition of ochre. Commercial artists force the highlights for the sake of reproduction.

HANDS

Hands should be well drawn and composed in a relaxed and easy manner. So often one sees hands painted in a forced, strained, and too fancy pose. Constantly look up at the face as you paint the hands. The skin tones should match, and the proportions be related. Don't paint red fingernails; years from now they may look silly. As far as I am concerned they add nothing to the hands, and as a fashion I deplore them.

COSTUME

The monotony of modern attire, the stark collar, drab coloring, and sameness of cut, creates a problem for today's portrait painter. The standardization of clean-shaven face, close-cropped hair, and unattractive clothing does not add up to interesting subject matter. When it is possible to have

72

DANISH GIRL *by Eugene Speicher, N.A. This artist was certainly one of America's finest portrait and figure painters and his pictures are in every important museum in the country. His distinctive style and personality make him a painter well worth studying.* (Courtesy Whitney Museum.)

a subject pose in a more casual costume, such as hunting clothes, fishing togs — anything except a well-pressed business suit — the resulting portrait is far more interesting and the accessories contribute both to the design and coloring of the painting.

There is a great deal more variety of coloring, texture and style in women's dress. An extreme style, of course, will look pretty funny some years hence, but by choosing an unchanged style with care — and there are many such styles — the painter can avoid this hazard.

Paint the costume and accessories as you would a still life, giving movement and design to the dark and light of the folds. Make the folds express the body underneath. You can do this only by studying carefully the basic folds which clothing always takes, with variations. Don't just swish in the darks but paint everything in the canvas as beautifully as you would the head.

If you have painted still life you will do this. Many portrait painters slight the accessories and it is easy to spot those who are only interested in the portrait aspect and care nothing about making the picture beautiful and complete from top to bottom. Take a good old master and cut out any square inch of canvas and you will find it beautifully painted.

BACKGROUNDS

In the beginning a student will be satisfied with almost any kind of background, and I realize that he is really progressing when he becomes conscious of the great importance of a suitable background. A background must always act as a complement to your picture, never as an obstruction. I have come to the conclusion after years of painting that the simpler you keep the background the better. So many feel that they must tell some kind of story in the background. This, of course, detracts from your portrait and is a literary point of view which does not appeal to me. I don't want to know exactly what the background tells me except that it is there and feels right with this picture. The eye needs a rest in the simpler open spaces in the canvas. Try to get a feeling of air behind the figure and not a cut-out-of-oilcloth effect. Avoid repetition of the same color in each picture. The problem you solve in one painting will not do for any other.

I find there is a tendency to repeat in the background the colors that appear elsewhere in the portrait. This produces a tonal, uninteresting, and dull

AMISH GIRL   *appears in the permanent collection of the*
Sarasota Art Association. The Amish are very shy about posing,
but I managed to get this little seven year old to pose for a short time.

ELLA STAHL   *I painted Mrs. Stahl, the wife of the illustrator and fine artist Ben Stahl, in Sarasota, Florida several years ago. (Collection of Ben Stahl.)*

picture. I try to use a color that has no relationship to the rest of the picture but which will act as a complement to the whole.

I used to think it necessary to paint the background in the same color as that which actually appeared behind the model, but now I believe that a far better color probably can be invented. It is certainly your prerogative to select any color which suits your fancy. Some believe that the sitter's skin is influenced by the color of the background. I suppose this is true to some extent, but I prefer to improvise in an effort to find the most advantageous color for this particular portrait. Sometimes it is necessary to paint several different trial backgrounds before hitting on a suitable one.

SCRAPING

I am a firm believer in scraping as you paint from day to day. Not once but many times. Taking off with a palette knife the superfluous paint that inevitably builds up in painting makes the surface more workable, always simplifies, and often leaves the way open for improvement.

Just a light scraping will not remove as much paint as you would suppose. I scrape several times during the first sitting and always before I stop painting for the day. It is hard to get students to do this. They feel that if they have spent all that time applying the paint, they may lose something by scraping it off — even very lightly. You will not lose anything worth saving; rather, you will be able to build your paint where you want it heavier. In other words, you will be creating your own surface texture.

RETOUCHING VARNISH

On the second sitting the darks are usually pretty well dried in and need to be restored to their original depth and richness. It would be useless to work on the picture in this state without first blowing on a little retouching varnish, using either a mouth atomizer or the new push button pressure cans.

A common fault, hard to correct once the damage is done, is to blow on too much varnish. This produces an unworkable surface like oilcloth, too slick and shiny, and often the varnish will even run down, carrying some of your paint with it. Just a few light blows are enough to restore the original color, and you can work into the picture immediately without waiting for it to dry, provided, of course, you have not made the varnish too wet and soupy.

STEP 1 *The figure is quickly sketched in raw umber and turpentine. The only aim at this point is to place the portrait well within the allotted space. Everything else about the portrait is subject to change. Later, as you will see, the mouth will be eliminated. No charcoal is used and the size of the canvas is 20" x 24".*

78

STEP 2 *I am ready to block in the large areas of light and the approximate shape of the shadows. All half-lights and subtle modeling is for later construction. The hair in light and dark is also noted.*

79

STEP 3 *The eyes are roughed in and some further modeling of the dark areas is developed. At this point I took out the slight drawing of the mouth and painted a light skin tone over the place where the mouth will eventually be placed.*

STEP 4   *This was at the beginning of the second day. The model appeared with a slightly different hair-do which I thought more attractive, so another topknot was added. One eye has been further developed and the mouth tentatively placed.*

81

STEP 5 *The other eye is nearing completion and some of the modeling on the shoulders and chest is appearing.*

82

STEP 6 *More development of the head and features and more modeling of the body and the beginnings of the costume.*

STEP 7   *The head at this point is nearly complete but a good deal of work remains to be done on the body and costume.*

84

CIRCUS GIRL   *The model for the completed painting was an Italian circus girl, one of a famous family. It seemed to me that such a flamboyant creature with exotic hair coloring and sparkling costume called for an equally colorful and violent background.*

CHAPTER FIVE

PAINTING THE FIGURE

PAINTING AND DRAWING from the nude has been, and I suspect always will be, a most essential part of the knowledge a painter must have. The knowledge gained from its study is of inestimable value, especially for the artist whose aim is to paint portraits and the draped model. The painter or student of painting who is able to construct a sound nude figure will have no trouble giving his draped figures an illusion of solid flesh beneath the clothing.

Obviously it would be difficult to paint a well-modeled nude in beautiful glowing colors without a well-rounded knowledge of solid drawing; and certainly a knowledge of anatomy is essential.

LEARNING TO DRAW

The only way to learn to draw is by drawing. I have never discovered any short cut. Drawing from the nude is by far the best way to study the human figure: its structure, proportions, rhythm, and action. I know that this is not so easily accomplished unless one lives in a large city where professional models are readily available. Furthermore, hiring a model is costly. One good solution is to form a sketch group of a dozen or so serious students, who can share the expense of a model and meet to sketch in the evenings

END OF SUMMER   *Picture of a reluctant bather, painted in a chilly color scheme. Note the definite light and shadow on figure and observe how the line of the drapery opposes the vertical figure.*

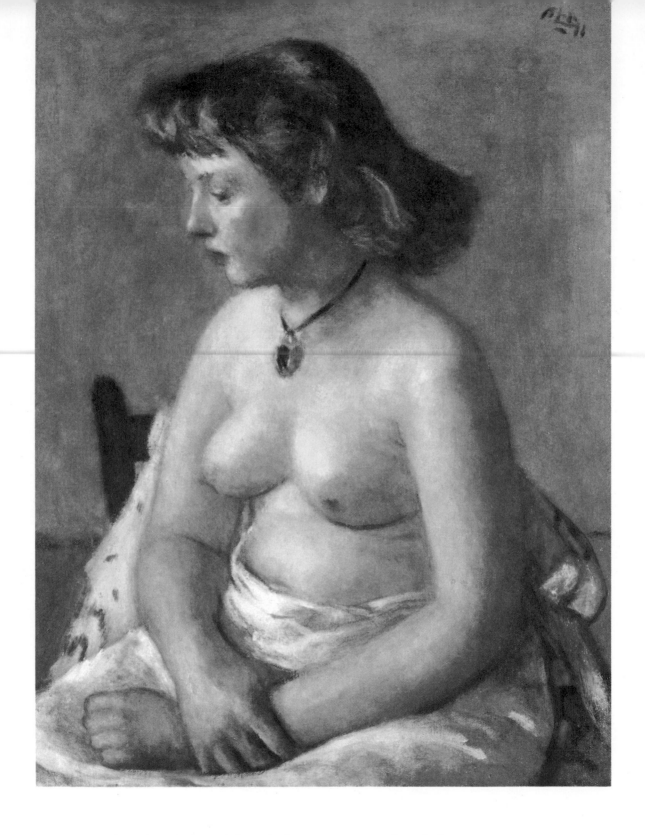

SEATED NUDE *by Robert Philipp.   I don't think anyone can paint the nude figure better than Robert Philipp. His adolescent girls are never sweet, insipid or sentimental. His handling of the skin in light and in shadow is superb.*

and weekends. If this is not feasible, you can still sketch from the clothed figure and learn a great deal.

Get a fairly large pad of newsprint paper at your local art materials store, plus several soft pencils, about 5B or even softer. Newsprint is inexpensive and is ideal for working with pencil. Later, you will want to buy charcoal and do more finished drawings on more expensive charcoal paper.

POSING THE MODEL

Quick action poses seem to be the best way to get movement, rhythm, and life into your drawing. Action poses of five or ten minutes are most valuable. Later, you can intersperse some longer poses for more careful study. As your drawing advances, you can use these longer poses to make the careful and detailed drawings which will help you to become proficient.

Pose the model so that there is good distribution of light and shadow. A strong light will give you a great contrast of light and shade, so that you can identify the forms easily.

OBSERVING THE MODEL

When you look at your subject, try to find the essential line that gives the figure rhythm and action. Let us say that you are drawing a nude back. Note the curve of the spine. If the model is standing with the weight on one foot, observe the reverse action of the shoulders and the hips: the shoulders will be high on one side and the hips will be just the reverse. At this moment, you are trying to capture the big lines of the movement. It is not necessary to labor over a finished drawing.

A five minute pose will give you enough time to express the essence of the figure. After doing many of these quick sketches, you will be surprised to see how much you will improve. Then try a few longer poses, allowing yourself more time to block in the large dark and light areas.

Keep all your sketches and review them now and then. You must be your own severest critic. Note where you have failed to translate the basic line and form. If your drawing is static and without movement, there is always a reason; find it.

SUGGESTIONS FOR FURTHER STUDY

It certainly won't hurt to learn as much anatomy as you can absorb. There are many good books on the subject: they will reward you if you study them conscientiously. You may even want to learn the names of the bones and the muscles, although the main thing is to learn their form and function.

I have found that practice in drawing from casts such as Michelangelo's popularly called *Muscle Man,* is very helpful in gaining a foundation in practical anatomy. This cast of a male figure stripped of the outer skin exposes for easy identification all the muscles of the entire figure and can be purchased in a size about eighteen inches high at almost any good art supply store. I believe everyone should have one on hand.

Go to museums and study the drawings of the masters. Buy good books of master drawings and build your own "museum without walls."

It is certainly true that no one draws well enough. There is always so much more to learn. If you are determined to learn to be a good draftsman, with constant practice you are bound to improve.

THE IMPORTANCE OF DRAWING

There is too little emphasis on fine drawing today. Far too many teachers tell students that it is no longer necessary to learn to draw in order to become a fine artist (possibly because the teachers themselves cannot draw). This, I think, accounts for the vast amount of mediocre and downright bad painting being produced today. If you study their drawings carefully, you will find that most of the masters of the modern idiom are sound draftsmen.

FIGURE PAINTING

When you draw, you work primarily with line. Of course, there is no line around anything in nature. Thus, when you paint the figure, you work more from masses of light and shade. Working in this way, you are able to solidify the forms and add another dimension to your work. The advice given in former chapters can be applied in painting the figure. The problems and approach are the same.

The great difference is that you do not concentrate on achieving a likeness. Figure painting, however, is the ultimate test of your ability to observe and draw the human form. A figure painting that is badly drawn is of little value and is a dead give-away: to the onlooker, it reveals what little knowledge and experience the artist really has. It all boils down to the simple statement I made a moment ago: the way to learn to draw is to *draw*.

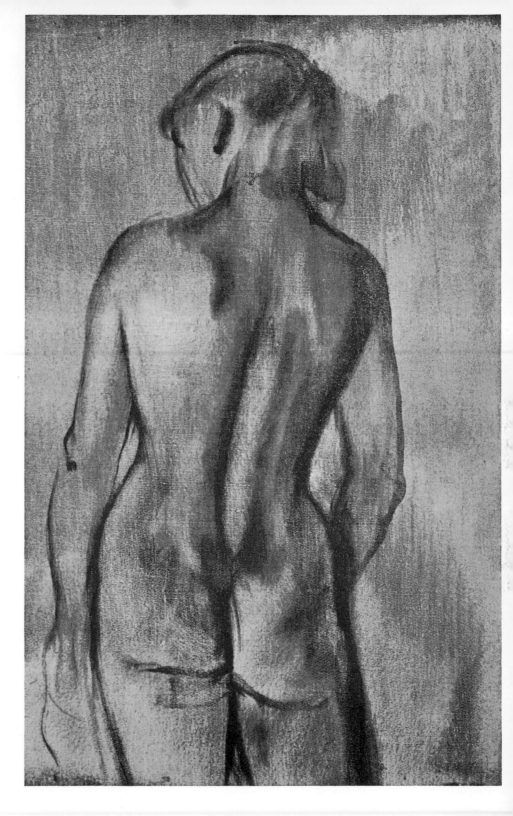

STEP 1 *Roughing in the standing pose on a 16" x 24" toned canvas. No effort is made to draw accurately, but accent is upon placing of figure on canvas.*

STEP 2 *The large mass of shadow and skin in light is blocked in. A note of red for the hair is added at this point. I am still not too concerned about exact drawing at this stage of the picture. A patch of light color to show limits of hair is sketched in.*

STEP 3 *Developing the modeling of shadow and light masses. The light and dark of the hair is patterned and a little more attention is given to the face and ear at this stage.*

STEP 4 *The head in lost profile is nearing completion, with some further developing of shadows and light areas. Ear is nearly completed.*

94

STEP 5 *Torso and head nearly completed. A little more background is brushed in, leaving the hand and completion of background for the last pose.*

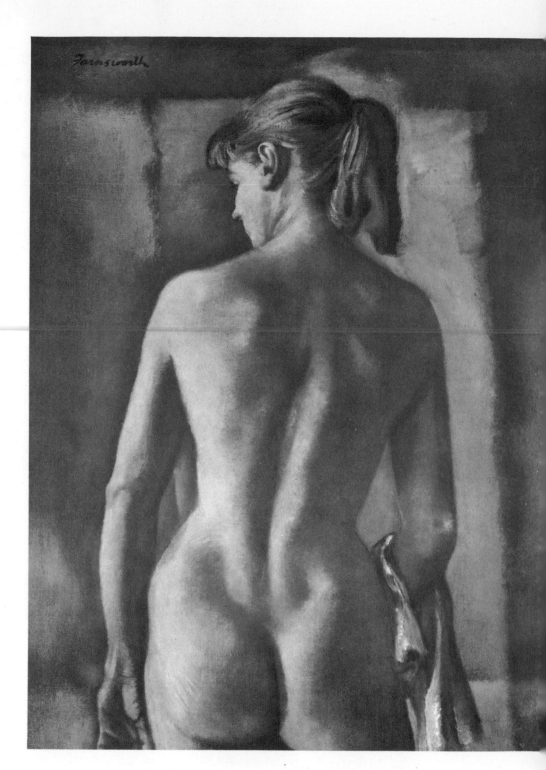

COMPLETED PAINTING
The hand was finished and the towel added to break an awkward pose of the arm next to the body. Background repainted in one sitting, with addition of opposing lines to give the picture better design. Shadows are pure raw umber with addition of white. Yellow ochre, raw umber, and a lot of white made up the skin in light.

96

Once you have learned the fundamentals of figure drawing, you will find that they become part of your subconscious. You will know instinctively — without stopping to analyze — whether the forms, proportions and anatomy of a figure are accurate. You will literally *sense* whether or not a drawing is convincing. You will be able to study the model for a brief moment, locate the dominant lines of the pose, and set the figure down on paper or canvas with decisive strokes.

Drawing, of course, can be an end in itself. A good drawing is an independent work of art, not merely a preliminary study for a painting. But for the portrait and figure painter, drawing must ultimately become part of the process of painting. It is often helpful to make one or more drawings of a pose — in pencil, charcoal, or Conté crayon — before you begin painting. The purpose of these preliminary drawings is to analyze the figure and solve the basic problems of composition.

On the other hand, seasoned painters often plunge right in and begin work directly on the canvas. For these artists, drawing has already become second nature. As one great artist has said: "You will *really* know how to draw when you no longer have to *think* about drawing."

CHAPTER SIX

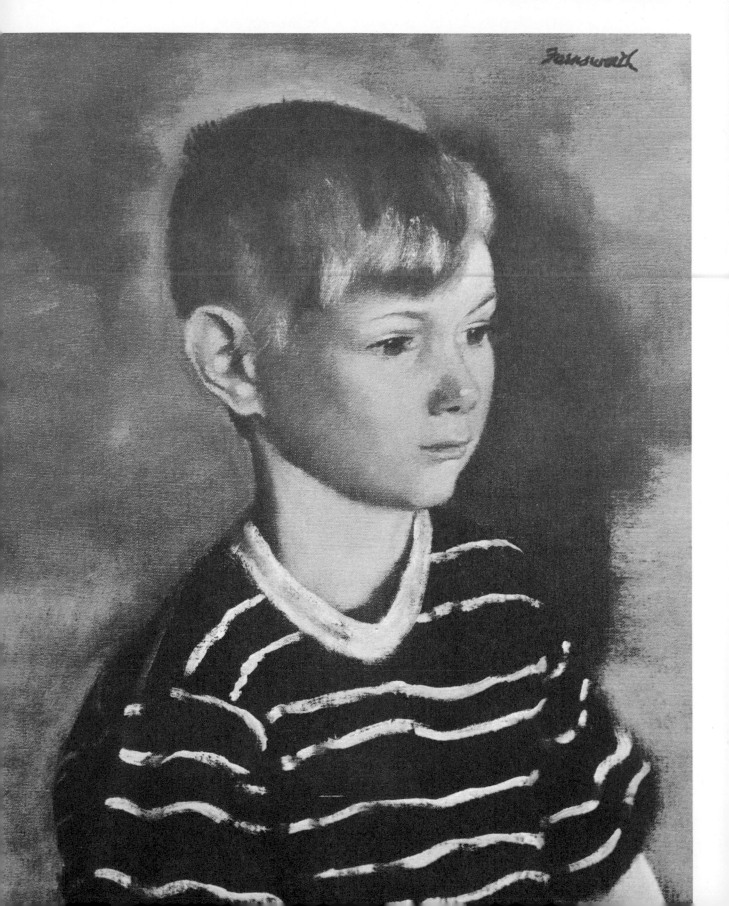

SO YOU WANT TO BE
A PORTRAIT PAINTER

WHAT IS A PORTRAIT? A portrait is a work of art representing an individual. This is as good a definition as any, though it represents the ideal. In too many instances, however, portraits fall far short of this. Too often a portrait is a likeness only, and a flattering one at that, devoid of any artistic or esthetic value, a formula, a hack job. A commercial portrait painter considers a portrait commission a picture painted for gain only, one which has satisfied the client and for which he has been paid — regardless of how he feels about the portrait personally.

This need not and should not be the case. So many great portraits in the past have been commissioned and yet, because of the artist's integrity and ability, have become lasting works of art.

The indifference and ignorance on the part of a great number of people who commission portraits are responsible for the poor standard of work being done now. Most people simply cannot distinguish between a good portrait and a bad one and appear to be interested only in a flattering likeness.

I have been asked to look at too, too many of these pictures in my lifetime, and no adjective can describe the awfulness of these pictures that people have paid good money for.

The tenth-rate painter, who by no stretch of the imagination can be dig-

PORTRAIT OF A YOUNG BOY   *The delicacy of the head is emphasized by the strong dark of the polo shirt.*

nified by the name artist, has gotten away with it time and time again. The unhappy part is that there are many exceedingly good portrait painters who could have been commissioned in his place who would have painted a very good portrait if the client only had enough knowledge and taste, or lacking these, had taken advice from someone who had.

Nine times out of ten these commercial painters work from photographs. This is the only way they know how to work. Being given a sitter to paint would simply stump them. With an enlarged photograph and some tracing paper they are in their elements.

On the brighter side of the picture, there are many people with taste and discernment who commission portraits from good painters and in consequence have lasting, dignified and charming pictures to show for the money spent.

A friend of mine, who is a very good commercial photographer, told me not long ago that color photography was so good now that it would surely put all portrait painters out of business. This statement, which is entirely untrue, is also absurd. Have you ever visited anyone's house and seen an enlarged color photograph on the wall, say over the mantelpiece? Of course not. I don't believe anyone would be guilty of such bad taste.

PORTRAITS AND PERSONALITY

A good portrait is such a personal thing — an interpretation of the subject, a distillation of personality — that it is silly even to defend it against whatever even the best camera can produce. This does not mean photography hasn't its place, but it can never compete, in a true sense, with a painting that is also a work of art.

A portrait is never an exact thing. It is a mood, a composite of a person. No man has an eye or hand accurate enough to set down to the fraction of an inch the features of a face or dimensions of a head. Let the camera do this. The camera does not lie, but it sees only what is on the surface and this it records mechanically. A painter probes deeply into the personality of his subject. He sees the head as a person does — accenting the proper places, drawing out the hidden quality which must be *felt* as well as seen.

When one is painting a portrait it is difficult to keep in mind that, while a likeness is important — and certainly one owes the client the finest and most

THE PREACHER AND THE HAWK   *The young pastor of a Provincetown*
church posed for this portrait in which I endeavored to
express both repose and turmoil.

DETAIL FROM WHITE FLOWER *by John Carroll, N.A.*
This artist painted his subjects with great simplicity and restraint
of color. The end results were highly personal and very beautiful.

sympathetic likeness that is within his capabilities to produce — he also owes himself the satisfaction of producing as fine a painting as he can achieve with the experience and equipment at his command. It is possible that his patron will cherish the picture only for its likeness, but many years from now who will care whether or not it resembled the sitter faithfully, or even who he was? The picture will survive only if it is a great work of art.

For the conscientious painter the only satisfactory portrait is one which, mainly, pleases himself. This he has been allowed to create without any outside interference. There are intelligent people who realize this, and it is in their houses that one finds really good portraits.

Sargent said that it was impossible to please more than two members of a family, and he was quite right. People who are totally unqualified to judge will not hesitate to tell you instantly what is wrong with a portrait. This might be a real help, but unfortunately each member has a different idea. If you were to accept all the suggestions offered and make all the proffered corrections, you would have a sorry-looking thing as a result.

Let us face facts; some people are simply not paintable. As Gilbert Stuart so vehemently pointed out, it is difficult to make much of a silk purse from some subjects.

However, it has been my experience that no matter how unattractive the sitter, one can find something unique that will at least give the portrait dignity and personality, if not physical beauty. I try to feel that such subjects pose a definite challenge which must be met and solved. With this attitude it is surprising what rewarding results can be achieved.

Color, costume and accessories beautifully painted are a great help when added to a well-painted head. This is where the good painter shines and where the fake always falls down. No amount of flattery or adornment will help if this is all you have been able to produce in your picture.

An artist friend of mine painting a past-middle-aged dowager told me that she complained, "Oh, Mr. Jones, do I look that old and that fat?" This, mind you, after he had taken twenty years and twenty pounds off the portrait. It makes you wonder.

BEGINNING YOUR CAREER

How does one, especially a young portrait painter just beginning his career, get started in his chosen profession?

MARJORY *by Ejnar Hansen. This portrait is notable*
for the lively texture of its brush strokes and
passages applied with the palette knife.

Let us assume that you have reached the point where you can paint and draw well enough so that your portraits are technically assured and you can achieve a respectable likeness. Ask someone who interests you as a subject to pose for you. Paint this person with all the ability at your command, and paint it for *yourself,* without thought of pleasing the sitter or of selling it to him. In this way you will concentrate all your facility in making it, as nearly as you can, primarily a work of art.

If the sitter or his family shows an interest in the finished picture, oftentimes a purchase price can be arranged which will be entirely agreeable. If the sitter, on the other hand, manifests no interest in owning the portrait, there is no embarrassment whatsoever; you have had an interesting model and acquired a picture which you may want to exhibit or sell to someone else.

PRICING YOUR WORK

There are thousands of people with modest incomes who are longing to have good portraits of members of their families, especially if there are children, who can afford to pay a few hundred dollars for a picture. If a young painter is satisfied with a modest fee — and he should be at this point in his career — he will probably have all the commissions he cares to accept because one satisfactory portrait almost invariably leads to others. But he must do his best and not let anyone either pay for, or keep, a portrait that does not entirely satisfy his sitter or sitter's family. It is better to start an entirely new one, or abandon the project altogether, than leave behind a picture which will find its way to the attic. The money he receives can in no way repair the harm done to his future reputation by a bad picture.

There is no better way for a young painter who has talent and can paint a good head to make his way than by painting portraits, and he gains invaluable experience while doing so.

It would be difficult to name any profession that hasn't its drawbacks, and I have tried to point out the difficulties which are inherent in the painting of portraits. I, for one, find it much more rewarding than other subjects. The deep satisfaction of setting down on canvas, for all time, the personality, charm, beauty or dignity of the subject and the pride the painter feels in his accomplishment are compensations that all creative people feel are reward enough.

CHAPTER SEVEN

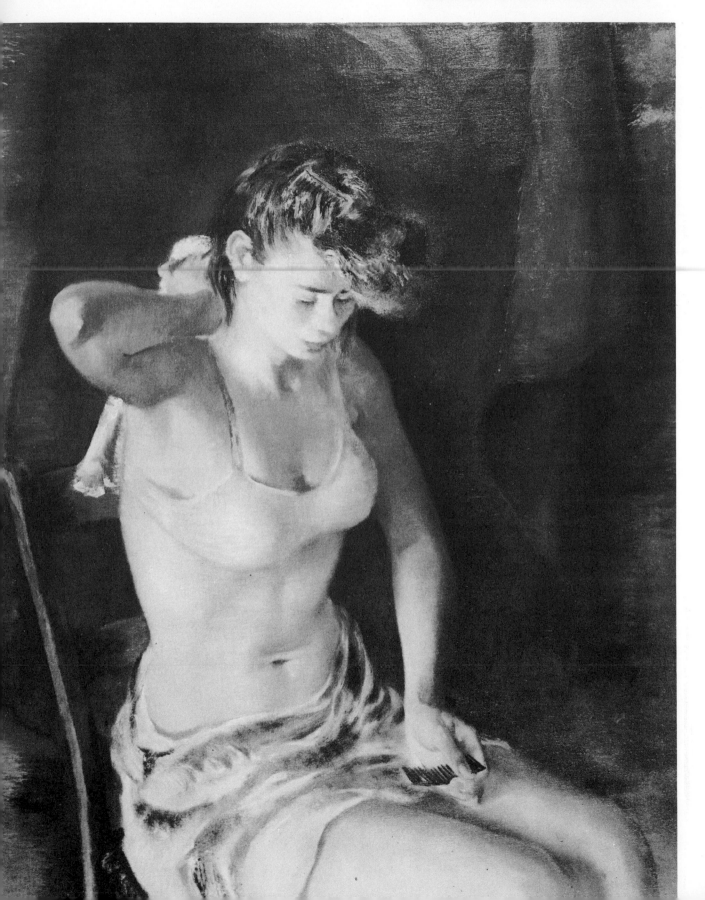

MORE ABOUT PIGMENTS

THE FOLLOWING NOTES on pigments are in the form of answers to questions posed by my students in both my North Truro, Massachusetts and Sarasota, Florida classes. They are reproduced here in question and answer form as they were taken down in shorthand by a class member:

Q. *Aside from the basic palette which is ideal for beginners, what about some of the new colors that have appeared on the market in the last few years?*

A. There are times when in order to produce especially brilliant colors, such as emerald green and Prussian blue, you will feel the need of adding extra pigments to your basic palette. There is a beautiful emerald green tint on the market (made from phthalocyanine pigment), which is very pure and transparent. The emerald green (aceto arsenate) is extremely poisonous and fugitive in mixture with sulphurous colors, such as cadmiums and ultramarine. A phthalocyanine blue sold under such trade names as Rembrandt and Winsor blue are like Prussian blue and have the same powerful tinting ability but are far more permanent.

Q. *You recommend oxide of chromium (green) so highly; just where do you find a use for it?*

A. Eugene Speicher introduced me to this color some years ago. I use it in many places and love the color. In skin that is in shadow, it is especially

GIRL COMBING HER HAIR   *This presented a difficult problem in the foreshortening of the raised arm. It was painted in Florida. The color scheme is flesh color and pink.*

valuable mixed with Venetian red. It gives a warm violet glow to a shadow, though it sometimes has to be warmed with the addition of yellow ochre. It is a very powerful color and only a small amount is necessary. It is one of the most permanent colors, one that is sadly neglected.

Q. *I noticed when I visited your studio last summer that you had a curious pink color on your palette. What is this color and how do you use it?*

A. The color you saw, believe it or not, is called "flesh tint." While it could under no circumstances be used directly from the tube to produce flesh color, I find it valuable in admixture with yellow ochre and green in producing the subtleties of skin in light. Of course one could mix it, but it is handy to have it ready-mixed in a tube. Made by Winsor & Newton, it has become very popular lately but you may not find it in your art supply store.

Q. *I am interested in knowing at least a little about the ordinary colors that I use every day. Could you tell me what they are and where they come from?*

A. I, too, am interested in knowing about the ordinary colors which are so familiar to us and I think a little information about them adds to our enjoyment in their use.

Yellow and brown ochres are earth colors which contain iron hydroxide. The natural ochres are more or less impure and contain, among other things, humus, clay and organic matter. The brilliance and hue of these pigments are often due to the impurities, but washing is necessary to free the natural pigment from these impermanent mixtures. Therefore, it is necessary to rely upon your color maker to furnish you with only the best quality ochres. Simply because a pigment is an earth color is not a guarantee that it will be permanent unless great care is taken in its manufacture. The best ochres comes from France, though some are obtained from the Harz Mountains in Germany. The ochres cover fairly well and require on an average of about sixty percent oil, and are among the most useful and permanent colors on an artist's palette.

The Mars colors, yellow, orange, violet, etc. are more transparent than the natural ochres, but they must also be well washed. They are valuable colors and, to my way of thinking, too little used.

Some authorities do not recommend raw sienna as an oil pigment because

NUDE *by John Koch, N.A. This artist is
intrigued by the glowing skin of the undraped
figure. He generally places his models in their
natural settings.*

it requires such an enormous quantity of oil (up to 200 percent). This is supposed to lead to rapid darkening, especially in underlayers. It is considered unobjectionable in other techniques. The best raw sienna is found in Tuscany and in the Harz Mountains.

Naples yellow was known to the old masters; it contains lead antimoniate and as a lead color is a good dryer with excellent covering quality, though very poisonous. There is a belief that Naples yellow should not be allowed to come in contact with a steel painting knife as it will cause discoloration, but there seems to be little evidence that this is true. Also the belief that Naples yellow should not be mixed with the iron colors, such as the ochres, has proved false. It requires very little oil, only about fifteen percent, and is absolutely permanent when pure.

The lighter tones of the chrome colors do not stand up well in light, often turning grayish green. Since we now have the beautiful and permanent cadmiums, there seems to be little point in using the chrome colors at all.

Zinc yellow, while still extensively used by many painters, also turns green and, therefore, should be replaced by cadmium yellow light.

Both barium yellow and strontian yellow have a better reputation than zinc yellow, but when ground in oil they discolor slightly and have a greenish cast. No need to use either one.

Cadmium yellow is the most valuable yellow on an artist's palette and when put up by a reliable manufacturer who produces it undiluted without admixture with chrome yellow, is a completely permanent and brilliant color. It should not be mixed with the copper colors such as emerald green, as it will turn permanently black. No one in his right mind would use emerald green anyway, so this would seem to be an unnecessary warning.

Hansa yellow is a new coal tar pigment which is very permanent and brilliant.

Indian yellow need not concern us here as it is very expensive and often diluted. It is made from the urine of cows that have been fed on mango leaves and comes from Monghyr, a city in India.

Cobalt yellow is a mineral color often used as a substitute for Indian yellow; it is very expensive and is superfluous.

Gamboge is used in watercolor; it is not light-proof and as an oil color is unusable.

Red iron oxides, known as English, Indian, Venetian red, and light red are all absolutely permanent. They cover and dry well and require from forty to sixty percent oil. The Mars reds also belong in this group.

Burnt sienna requires about eighteen percent of oil and sometimes it jells in the tube. This color can be used in all techniques and is a fiery glazing color.

Vermilion is a chemical compound of mercury and sulphur and is slightly poisonous. It turns black when exposed to light. The cadmium reds are far more stable and there seems to be little point in using a vermilion today.

Cadmium red, like all the cadmiums, is completely permanent. Cadmium red light and cadmium red deep should be used by any artist who wishes to paint with a permanent palette.

Madder lake is made by boiling the root of the madder plant; the extract is precipitated on a clay base and produces a beautiful though impermanent transparent red.

Alizarin crimson is an artificial coal tar product and in permanency exceeds the natural rose madder. All the alizarins are fairly serviceable and sufficiently light-proof for general purposes. The other lakes, called yellow, brown, and blue should not be used.

Carmine is made from the cochineal insect. It is a beautiful red but is too impermanent for use.

Q. *Why do art dealers stock impermanent colors when there are permanent colors which are better and cost no more?*

A. Because there is a demand for them; it is as simple as that. If the dealer does not sell you what you ask for, another will, although I should imagine he would much rather furnish you with permanent colors.

Here are some of the substitutions that should be made for impermanent colors: Rembrandt blue or any other good make instead of Prussian blue. Rembrandt green and Rembrandt emerald green tint instead of emerald green. Rembrandt brown instead of Vandyke brown. Cadmium yellow instead of chrome yellow or zinc yellow. Cadmium red instead of vermilion.

Q. *What about white lead versus zinc white?*

A. There seems to be a good deal of confusion among students and painters — and also a certain amount of controversy — as to the relative advantages of white lead and zinc white.

White lead, flake white, cremnitz white, and blanc d'argent are basic lead carbonate. The old Dutch process of making white lead was to suspend strips of lead rolled into spirals in covered earthenware jars containing acetic acid. The pots were buried under tanner's bark or dung, the heat generated by the fermentation caused an increase in the amount of carbonic acid. The white powder thus formed on the metal as a coating was white lead. Much depended on the purity of the lead used. It is said that the Venetian old masters exposed the lead powder to the air in sacks for a year before using and washed it well to free it of all acid and sugar of lead.

In the grinding process, the lead is first mixed to a heavy, cream-like consistency with water, later the oil is added, which forces the water out. It requires very little oil, only about fifteen percent.

The advantages of white lead are its great covering power and its good drying quality. It is never necessary to add siccatives to white lead in order to quicken its drying.

White lead is compatible with all the necessary colors on an artist's palette, although it may darken with poorly made cadmiums. Though some authorities state that white lead, ultra-marine, and vermilion do not stand up well together, there seems to be no real evidence that this is true. Artists who wish to avoid vermilion may substitute cadmium red light.

The greatest drawback of white lead is that it is very poisonous. Some doctors claim it can be absorbed through the skin and many have been poisoned who have inhaled white lead dust. White lead also yellows when kept in the dark; however, it will lose its yellowish cast if again exposed to a strong light.

Zinc white, blanc de zinc, Chinese white (zinc oxide) was introduced as an artist color about 1840 and was unknown to the old masters. As a powder it is much looser, bulkier and requires about twice as much oil as white lead. It is much colder in appearance and covers less well. It is also more

HAPPY CHILD *A young Irish girl who was indeed a happy child. A collector in New Britain, Connecticut is the owner.*

brittle than white lead and not as suitable as an underpainting ground. Zinc white does have the advantage of being nonpoisonous and does not yellow. A mixture of lead white and zinc white should possess all the good and none of the bad qualities of both pigments.

Titanium white, which is titanium dioxide, is a comparatively new pigment. It has great covering power and is nonpoisonous. It is especially valuable in watercolor and tempera, but is said to yellow when mixed with oil. Pure titanium is sometimes cut with zinc white to increase its drying power and to prevent it from yellowing.

Used sensibly, any of these whites are suitable for the artist's palette. Weighing the advantages and disadvantages of each, a painter must decide for himself which ones meet his needs. I have always used zinc white and see no reason to switch.

Q. *You think you have the formula for the underpainting material which Rembrandt used? Is this a secret or will you divulge it?*

A. Yes, I think I do have an approximation of the formula. The reason I think so is because it was given to me by a Belgian whose grandfather was associated with Block, the Belgian manufacturers of artists' colors. He analyzed a damaged Rembrandt in an effort to discover the exact formula. I have this recipe and it is no secret. I worked with this underpainting material for two years and why I no longer use it is another long story. I did not give it up, however, because it was an unsatisfactory material. The pictures I did during that period have not shown the slightest deterioration.

It is a difficult formula to work with and I do not necessarily recommend it. It is, however, a fascinating technique and well worth exploring for those interested in various underpainting methods.

This particular recipe has been copied by a paint maker and is put up in tubes. I know the formula has been changed; whether it has been improved or not I cannot say, as I have not tried it. With my recipe one must mix a new batch every day, because it hardens overnight and is unusable the next day.

When painted on a hard surface, either board or canvas-mounted board, it will not crack, check or change in any way and will harden to such a degree that it cannot be scratched with a fingernail. Because of its brittle quality, it is easy to see that a flexible canvas would never do, hence the necessity of mounting.

The formula. Take lead white, mix with precipitated chalk, one-half of each. This chalk can be obtained at almost any drug store as it is the base of most toothpastes and powders. Wet the mixture of lead and chalk with Valentine's spar varnish, work together well with a spatula, adding only enough varnish to make a thick gummy mass about the consistency of the flake white as it comes out of the tube. Best not to mix too much as it will not keep, and a new batch can be put together in a matter of minutes.

The technique. Start laying in your composition in monotone. I generally add a little viridian to give the underpainting some definite form. Keep the monotone pale, however. In a portrait, for instance, keep the shadow areas very thin and load the lights with thicker impasto, modeling the head with your customary brush technique. This cannot be hurried and, of course, the immediate results will not look too promising, but do not be too hasty to start glazing until all your surfaces have been well thought out in advance.

Allow a couple of days for the undercoating to dry before beginning the glazes. For a glazing medium, I use one-third turpentine, one-third linseed oil, and one-third spar varnish.

Spar varnish is a pretty dark varnish and I wouldn't be surprised if you could find a paler varnish that would do just as well and still harden properly.

I use only the transparent colors for glazing and instead of doing much wiping off, I use the palm of my hand and fingers to work the glaze in. Doerner says that the old masters used their fingers as much as they did brushes, and I can easily see why.

Well, there you are. It's the darnedest stuff to work with; it's stringy, sticky, messy, difficult to control and exasperating, but I love it and the end results are sometimes unbelievably beautiful.

CHAPTER EIGHT

WHAT EVERY YOUNG PAINTER SHOULD KNOW

AT ONE TIME or another I have been asked a great many questions, not necessarily about painting but certainly directly connected with it.

There are many questions that are recurrent and I wondered if the answers to some of them might not be of help to most students. So I have put this chapter in the form of questions and answers, the first of which is:

Q. *I would like to study painting but there is the question of money. What about scholarships?*

A. There are many scholarships open to students of ability and industry. You can compete by submitting examples of your work in competition with others.

For those whose work is not yet up to this high a standard, there are monitorships (which are working scholarships) available at most art schools. These scholarships are most common and, I believe, most satisfactory both from the school's position and the student's.

I never give a straight scholarship to a student, for I believe it is not appreciated unless worked *for*. Most of my best pupils have been monitors, for they are generally the most ambitious and the hardest workers.

The duties of a monitor are not difficult. He is in charge of the class during the absence of the instructor, keeps order, poses the model, settles

NUDE BACK *I painted this almost in monotone, using only raw umber and white.*

117

disputes between pupils as to position, etc. After the painting class, he usually has the job of cleaning up — at least in most private art schools — and making himself generally useful. For this he receives free tuition and oftentimes much free extra criticism and advice from his teacher.

Q. *How do I know whether I have enough ability or enough interest to pursue a career in art?*

A. As to ability, this is difficult to answer. Some students show great ability in the very beginning, while others are slow starters and like the tortoise and his competitor often finish the race ahead of a brilliant starter.

A good teacher can generally tell if the student has enough promise or not, but it is quite a responsibility for him to advise whether one should make painting a life's work.

If you question whether you have enough interest, it is obvious by the question that the answer is no. Go into some other work which is all-absorbing to you. To want to pursue an art career is like being in love, you will know if this is it.

Q. *How can I make my way while I am studying painting?*

A. Just as you would if you were working your way through college, by turning your hand to any work that will leave time for painting. It doesn't matter what kind of work you do as long as it is honest and you earn enough while learning your profession to keep you going.

I have had students who mowed lawns, painted homes, and waited on tables in their off hours. There is also a deep satisfaction in earning your own way and these are the students I am most interested in.

Q. *If I am to succeed at painting now, won't I have to associate myself with the modern movement?*

A. No. It is true that the people who have gotten on the "band wagon" appear to have most of the success in being accepted in exhibitions — even the know-nothings. You should realize, however, that fashions in art come and go, but that good painting will always be good painting.

Probably the most successful painter in America today is Andrew

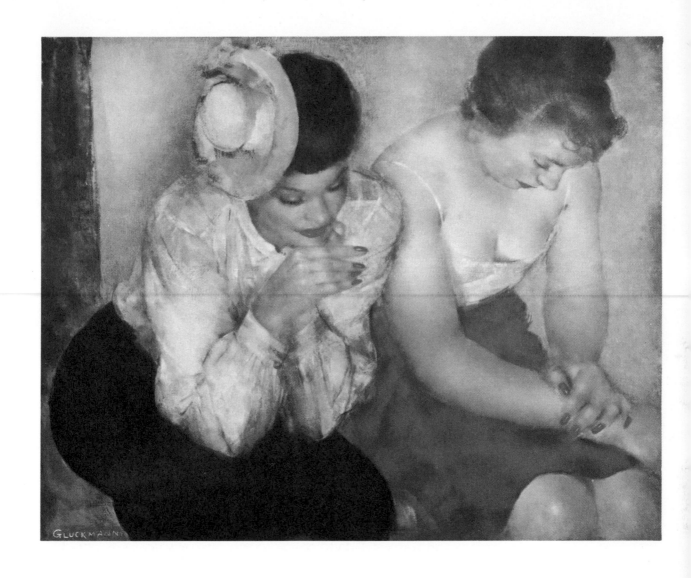

CONFIDENCES *by Grigory Gluckmann. In this study of two
seated figures, the painter has solved a complex problem
in composition. Note the delicacy of the flesh tones.*
(Courtesy Dalzell Hatfield Galleries)

Wyeth, who has consistently painted in his own individual, sound way and has not been seduced by the wave of abstractionism and nonobjective painting which has washed over this country in the last two decades.

At this writing a picture of his sold for a record price of $54,000 to a museum, and there are people waiting in line for any picture he will produce from now on. There are many other painters, perhaps not so well known, who have not been tempted into painting pictures that might lead to immediate but temporary success. One thing is certain, there is very little competition in paintings such as these, whereas every other amateur is painting psuedo-modern pictures which good modern painters must compete against.

If you genuinely feel the need to express yourself in the modern idiom, do so by all means. As long as you are sincere and honest in your expression you will not be a faker and a liar. This is the important thing.

Q. *Someone wants to buy a picture I painted in class. How much shall I ask?*

A. Oh my, how often have I been asked this question! I used to suggest a price but found from past experience that this was disappointingly low to the student, so I no longer do so. I think a student should be thankful for anything he can get for his pictures during his years of study. After all, there will be many more where that one came from, and far better ones. Get what you can but don't make the mistake of putting too high a value on what, after all, is just student work.

Q. *When should I strike out on my own and no longer attend art school?*

A. I think you will know and certainly your teacher will. But don't make the mistake of believing you know it all too soon. Far too many students

JENNY   *This was inspired by Robert Nathan's beautiful book, "Portrait of Jenny."*

stop school long before they are ready. One must be a student all one's life, seeking, learning, experimenting and perfecting.

Renoir at 76, painting a still life of anemones (the last picture he was ever to paint), remarked to someone who helped him unclasp the brush from his poor, crippled hand, "I think I am beginning to understand something about it."

Q. *What about correspondence courses in painting?*

A. They are of some value, no doubt, and have gotten many people started in painting who would otherwise not have done so. Aside from the fact that they are pretty expensive, they cannot possibly take the place of classroom instruction from a good teacher.

The stimulation, the competition, the greater amount of criticism and advice one gets from day to day from a teacher ready at hand will unquestionably advance a student further and quicker than if he were working alone and at a distance from his instructor.

Q. *Do you think a student should paint landscape even if he intends to be a portrait painter?*

A. I most certainly do. Why should you confine yourself to one kind of subject matter? Working out-of-doors should improve your color and give you an entirely different point of view. No exact drawing is necessary, so that you can concentrate on color, contrast, and the brilliance of sunlight.

Choose your subject carefully, try working against the light so that your picture will have great contrast and pattern.

The problem is the same as in still life. Match your patches of color, one against the other, while seeing all in a big way, avoiding detail, seeing variety of pattern, variety of color and a casual composition.

Who knows, you may become enamored of landscape, as so many of my students have, and wish to paint more and more of it. After all, it is a very pleasant and rewarding occupation.

One of the delights of landscape painting is the adventure of setting forth to find a subject. The landscape painter is preoccupied with such elemental things as weather and light. He feels the heady challenge of picking something to paint from all the welter under the sky.

Q. *Is it necessary to know the names of all the bones and muscles?*

A. It would certainly help one in the study of anatomy, and, make no mistake, anatomy is very important if one is to be a competent figure painter.

Many of the old masters spent years in the dissecting room, learning at first hand what lies beneath the outer skin, where the muscles spring from and to what they are attached. A good draftsman simply must be aware of these things; otherwise his figures will look ludicrous.

Q. *I was told by my former teacher that it wasn't necessary to go through all this business of learning to draw and paint, that I should express myself in my pictures without having to waste time on this.*

A. I am sorry to say that I have heard this tale before, too. I am afraid it is about the worst advice a teacher can give. How can one have too much knowledge of drawing and painting? The trouble is that some young students have had some small success in being accepted in a local exhibition by a work that is patently a fake modern. This, of course, leads him to believe that the discipline and hard work necessary to learn the craft of painting are something he can skip.

A wise man once said that knowledge and fine craftsmanship have never yet hampered genius.

CHAPTER NINE

CLASSROOM NOTES

I distrust talent. While it is valuable to have, it must be worked at. More valuable is the overwhelming urge to work and create day after day.

> ¶

Seeing and feeling are much more important than technical acrobatics. There is such a thing as having too much facility. Bear in mind that your work is admired for its content rather than technique.

> ¶

The young are bold and unafraid; it is a pleasure to teach them because they have nothing to unlearn. One of the hardest things to combat is bad teaching or teaching in which technique is stressed primarily.

> ¶

No matter how clumsy and uncertain you are in your technique, be sincere and use your ability of the moment to express, even in the simplest terms, what you feel and see.

> ¶

When I see some personal quality in a student's work I do everything I can to encourage it. We do not want everyone to paint alike.

ENRICA *My model, painted before the war, was a young Italian girl. The painting now hangs in a collection at Houston, Texas.*

ANNABELLA   *This picture, having strong contrasts in light and shade, is in the permanent collection of the Metropolitan Museum of Art, Arthur H. Hearn Fund.*

¶

Try to put down shadows and lights as nearly as possible in your first lay-in. It makes very little sense, to me, to make them wrong and waste time and effort correcting them.

¶

The subject matter is nothing compared to how you feel and see your material. The simplest subject becomes a work of art when seen through an artist's eyes.

¶

What good is technique if you have nothing to say?

¶

Of the two urges, for financial success or artistic success, the latter is the one to strive for. I don't know of any good painter who is not at least moderately successful financially. Some are even rich.

¶

Taste is something that is hard to give people. Some are born with it. A teacher must try to improve the others by example, study, and art education.

¶

All the colors on your palette are important. They cannot be obtained by mixing. That of course is why we use them.

¶

Always experiment. You will become stagnant if you repeat over and over what you already know.

¶

Don't try to paint exhibition pictures. If a good one comes out, fine. Always keep the humble attitude of a student as long as you paint.

¶

Don't calculate so much. Let your mind be informed by your eyes and heart.

¶

If you're not interested in your subject how do you expect anyone else to be?

¶

You ask me how to mix this or that color. I am not interested in that kind of teaching; furthermore, it would do you a disservice to show you any kind of formula. One person will arrive at a color in a totally different way from another person. I am always amazed at the way beginners achieve beautiful colors when they have very little knowledge.

¶

Discouragement is an occupational disease for art students. If you are discouraged keep it to yourself. I don't want to hear about it.

¶

Every painter I know is uneven. Don't be afraid of doing a flop; you are in good company.

¶

I think a teacher is not being fair to his pupils if he encourages them to paint as he does. I never demonstrate before a class; that is an easy way to teach, and all a student learns is to paint like his teacher. One is bound to lean on a teacher somewhat, this seems unavoidable, but I would much rather see one struggle on his own no matter how primitive the results.

¶

Painting is not all unadulterated fun. The best pictures are often those one sweats and swears over. Tell yourself that if it were easy anyone could have done it.

¶

Every teacher can teach you something. Fortunately, each has a different point of view. Accept what he has to offer and you will gain in the end.

¶

It is better to be in a class where at least some of the students are better than you are. You can learn much from them; you won't learn much from the others.

¶

A student may speak in words of one syllable if what he has to say is loud and clear and, best of all, if it is his own.

¶

If you load up the darks, the light catches the ridges of the impasto causing it to appear much lighter than it really is. Keep the darks flat. Load the lights if you will, but keep the darks simple.

¶

Using too much white gives a chalky look. The whole picture will look as though it had been to the laundry too often. You must consciously avoid dipping into the white pigment.

¶

If the paint builds up and becomes unmanageable, scrape it with a palette knife. A good habit. Scraping your picture pulls everything together, simplifies it, and leaves the way open for repainting and improving.

EASTER BONNET   *A very young girl proud of her new Sunday hat.*   129

NUDE BACK
by Leon Kroll, N.A.
This painter's popular
figure paintings are
respected for their sound
construction and solid,
sculptural quality.
(Courtesy Milch Gallery)

¶

Some edges are soft and some are hard; try to find which are which. All hard edges will result in a brittle, cut-out picture. All soft edges result in a picture seemingly out of focus.

¶

Keep things tentative to start with. Don't pin them down too soon. The best advice is to delay finishing.

¶

Colors at their fullest intensity are just one color; below the scale of primary colors there is an infinite variety of subtle, beautiful, subdued grays. Use intense color sparingly; make it point up and complement your grays.

¶

I must confess that I do not care much for the so-called pastel colors. Too sweet — though they have been handled on occasion by such a painter as Marie Laurencin, who seemed always to avoid a too saccharine quality. For my taste, give me the more profound, resounding colors away from the lavenders, baby pinks, and blues.

¶

What's wrong with black? So many students tell me that their former teachers forbade them to use it on their pictures. I suppose one can mix it, or an approximation of it, but to me black is a valuable, ready-made addition to any painter's palette. Note what the Dutch masters did with it.

¶

Too much medium results in paint that is too soupy. The effect on your picture is like the surface of oil cloth.

¶

Many painters, including myself, use no medium. You won't have much trouble with cracking if you use the paint just as it comes from the tube. If you must use a medium, one-third turpentine, one-third damar varnish, and one-third linseed oil is as good as any. Better not to use any.

¶

Try to avoid tonality — that is, a picture whose colors are too close in harmony. A picture needs the bite and sting of off colors. As in music, a monotonous harmony is relieved by a discord. This points up and enlivens the composition.

¶

Still life will teach you more than any other subject matter. Students who paint still life have very little trouble with portraits and landscapes. I can spot a person who has painted and loved still life the minute I see his picture. For one thing, his accessories are just as well painted as the head, not indifferently thrown together.

¶

Do not just copy. Interpret and translate in your own idiom. Your picture must be far more interesting than the subject before you. Let your personality come through. Don't see your subject through anyone's eyes except your own.

¶

A vigorous and personal still life, with much excitement going on, is a joy to see. Once you can successfully paint a still life, you should be able to handle any subject, nothing should scare you.

¶

The important thing is to paint the essence and distillation of a simple object.

¶

A still life is just too nice and polite if it doesn't talk back to me. Add a sour note, some tang and acidity; too much harmony is tiresome.

¶

All the rules of composition can be learned in a short time and broken. Composition is a matter of feeling, not calculation. If it feels right it is right.

¶

Color theory is for the birds. It's for people who can't think for themselves. Read about it, if you must, and then forget it.

¶

If you don't strain for a likeness, your portrait will nearly always come out better. I know from my own experience that if I am impatient to achieve a likeness too soon I sacrifice something as far as the painting goes.

¶

Pick out objects in a still life subject that are not beautiful or precious in themselves. Instead of using a silver platter, cut-glass wine bottle, beads and embossed book, go into the kitchen or to the town dump to find your subjects. It takes an artist's eye and hand to endow homely pieces with life and beauty. The artist's job is to show beauty in prosaic, everyday, common things.

Chardin was about the first to paint these kinds of subjects, and how beautifully he did it.

¶

Paint with a good fat brush well laden with pigment. Do not use oil paint like watercolor. Oil paint is an opaque medium. If it builds up and gets out of control, scrape it with your palette knife, leaving the way open for improvement.

¶

Give me the hard-working students rather than the talented ones any day. I went to school with many talented students but I don't know where they are today.

¶

Look out for highlights; be stingy with them. Don't make a head look as though it were sweating or had vaseline rubbed on its face. The highlights on the face should be very close in tone to the local over-all color.

¶

If you are doing a portrait commission you, of course, owe your client a good likeness, but you owe it to yourself first to produce a work of art. Even if your client doesn't care about this, you must.

¶

I have always felt that the inside of an oyster shell has more beauty than a string of precious beads, and is far more paintable.

¶

You have to educate yourself to love still life. Few students take to it in the beginning, but some grow to love it best of all.

¶

If you don't own a copy of *The Art Spirit* by Robert Henri, be sure to get a copy. It should be the Bible of all art students.

¶

If you didn't do so well this week — if the end result is not up to your expectations — perhaps you learned more than at any other time.

¶

There is a frightening gap between the conception and the execution. Bridge it as well as you can. I doubt if an artist is ever really satisfied with his picture, except perhaps the amateur who is pleased with everything he touches.

¶

Always have on hand canvases of various sizes. It is good to change around every so often, tall and thin, big and small.

¶

Don't give a hang what anyone thinks of your pictures. If your friends like them, well and good, but don't be distressed if they don't. Above all, please yourself first.

¶

I haven't any rules to give you about placing the head. You have to feel that it is right. I notice that after a while a student instinctively places his first drawing in the most pleasing composition and thereafter has little trouble.

¶

I don't mind if you tint your canvas; just be sure that it doesn't lead you into getting an over all low key. For some people an untinted canvas is best.

¶

Paint the lost profile just as though it were a still life. That is the way to do it. The features amount to nothing. It is certainly the best way to learn to paint portraits. Next week, move around more towards the profile where the features count for a little more. In this way you will soon be able to handle the head in any position.

¶

Model the planes and bony structure first as a sculptor would. See what happens around the temple, jaw, and eye socket. The poorest approach of all is to begin with the features and try to build a face around them.

¶

Jump around in your painting — a piece of color here and there so that you see the whole color scheme in your eye.

¶

It has often puzzled me how hard it is to paint simply and how easy it is to make your picture too complicated.

HELEN SAWYER   *A portrait of my wife, painted for the National Academy when she was made a member.*
(Collection of The National Academy.)

¶

One good thing about the modern movement in painting is that it opened the way for new and endless vistas and opportunities for exploration and development; but this includes, unfortunately, the opportunity to make fools of ourselves.

¶

Let your color express the form, instead of making your form and then coloring it.

¶

Do not be afraid of making mistakes, no picture was ever painted without them. If a happy accident occurs make the most of it, but do not try to make it happen again.

¶

I believe I can tell the mentality of a student by looking at his work, whether he was interested and excited or bored and lazy.

¶

The way you handle black shows your true ability as a painter — not merely to darken colors but to mix handsome grays. People who shun black miss out on a great deal.

¶

Do a lot of squinting at your model. It may give you crow's feet but it will be worth it. Everything is simplified and you won't see too much detail.

¶

Study carefully where the hair meets the flesh. Notice where the hair grows out of the skin, it is not hard and fast but soft and melting into the skin tone.

¶

Wrinkles are not just lines, they are tones, hard on one edge and soft on the other. You will never express it with hard lines.

¶

Don't paint the head too round. If you look more carefully you will find some angles and flat areas. Hardly anyone has a perfectly round head.

¶

When you are a master of advanced years you may learn what to leave out of the drawing of an eye. In the meantime put in everything you see there. This is the process of learning.

Q. *Do you believe in class demonstrations; that is, painting before the class?*

A. No, I don't. Many students have asked me why I do not do this. The answer is very simple. I know from my own experience as a student that when the teacher painted before the class, once a week, we all tried desperately to copy his technique and many of us succeeded. It took me many years to shake off these influences and I determined that I would not be guilty of the same thing.

It is natural to lean very heavily on your teacher's way of painting and I try to discourage this. Obviously some will copy your mannerisms as closely as possible. They are bound to see your work here and there but it is a form of flattery which does not appeal to me and does the student a great deal of harm. When I see a personal way of working I encourage this above every other asset I find in that student's work.

Demonstrations are an easy way to teach, but I believe they are a disservice to all students and lead to habits hard to overcome in later years.

Q. *Do you think one can learn to paint alone?*

A. Yes, I do, but it will take longer. Some very interesting work has been done by what we call primitives, who are self-taught. These painters have a child-like point of view and a very personal way of seeing things. Much primitive work is just plain bad but a few have made valuable contributions in the field of art.

For the student who can spare the time, there is nothing more valuable than class work. It is stimulating to work with others and one learns much from more advanced students, not to mention the teacher, who points out mistakes and guides him in the right direction. In this way progress is far more rapid and much of the discouragement which attends the worker alone is minimized.

It has been my observation that even a short period under a competent teacher will improve a student's work as much as 100 percent.

Q. *Can a person past middle age learn to become a competent painter?*
A. I have seen many who have. It would probably be a mistake to

make a career of painting at this age, but to want to create is a compelling force at no matter what age and I know many older people for whom painting has become their whole life interest. This interest has kept them young and alive both mentally and physically.

Doctors have known for years the therapeutic value of painting as a hobby and I have seen in my own classrooms an awakening of interest in a half-alive person which is amazing. Aside from the joy of creating something beautiful with their otherwise useless hands and minds, they have new eyes to see the wonders of beauty in the world that lies about us.

Q. *When does one feel ready to exhibit?*

A. In this country there are thousands of small art groups or associations. These are the places where you can first try out your wings. It is a wonderful experience to have a picture accepted at even the most humble exhibition, and if you should be so fortunate as to win an award, your joy knows no bounds. So send the first picture with which you feel you have excelled. Perhaps there is much left to be desired in it, and you must be your own severest critic, but when you see your picture in competition with others your critical sense will be keener and your desire to do better with your next picture will be aroused.

It is of course very disappointing to be turned down by a juried exhibition but instead of losing faith, get a little mad and show these people that on the next round you will make it.

Q. *Do you consider the list of paints you have suggested to be permanent?*

A. There is, of course, no such thing as absolute permanency, but these colors in any admixture should prove to be about as lasting as any. They should not fade or deteriorate over many hundreds of years if they are purchased from a reputable paint manufacturer.

However, no paints are any more permanent than the medium with which they are mixed and the support upon which they are painted. A poor

PRISCILLA   *A portrait of*
a little dark haired and lively eleven
year old, painted in Cape Cod several years ago.

138

medium and an inferior ground can ruin any picture, no matter how permanent the colors.

When I was a student nearly everyone in our class used a medium purchased in the school store. It was formulated from an ancient recipe and put out by a chemical firm. It was about the color and consistency of blackstrap molasses. I don't know what it contained but we all loved it. To our dismay, the pictures painted with it turned very dark in a few years, the paint cracked and some brown substance came to the surface and ran down the canvas. The first picture I sold to a museum done with this medium is in deplorable condition, cracked, darkened, and chipped. I shudder whenever I think of it and only wish I had known better at the time. That is why I suggest elsewhere that it is best to paint in the direct method without medium of any kind.

Q. *Is it necessary to paint the background the same color as the one behind the model in the pose?*

A. I used to think so, but now I believe that with experience you can invent a far better color than the one that happens to be there. There is a good deal of disagreement about this; some believe that the color of the skin is influenced by the color of the background in the pose and I suppose that this is true to some extent, but I prefer to experiment and find the most advantageous background, which will probably be totally different. Sometimes a background made up of many colors is the best one. The longer I work, however, the simpler I keep backgrounds. This also applies to the costume. It is certainly your prerogative to change the color of the dress to suit your preference and often it enchances the painting.

INDEX

Age, painting of, 55-56, 136; see also Features
Alcohol, 29
Anatomy, 89-90, 123; see also Features
Axis lines, 54-56; illus. of, 56

Backgrounds, 74-77, 85, 95, 140
Black, use of, 27-28, 131, 136; see also Colors, mixing of
Bones 60; see also Head, Nose
Books, reference, 24, 28, 133
Boxes (for paints), 21-24
Brackman, Robert, illus. by, 34
Brand names, 23, 33, 43, 107, 108
Brook, Alexander, illus. by, 62
Brushes, list of, 23; use of, 30-32; cleaning of, 31-33

Canvas, preparation of, 28-29, 32, 114-115; types of, 21, 28-29
Careers, 15-19, 103-105, 117-123, 124-138 *passim.*
Carroll, John, illus. by, 102
Charcoal, 21, use of, 39, 45, 54-56
Chalk, 115
Churchill, Sir Winston, 15
Colors, basic, 21-27; mixing of, 24-28, 39-41, 43, 63, 69, 96, 107-115, 127; origin of, 108-111; permanent, 21, 24-28, 107-111, 138-140; see also Black, White lead, Zinc white
Compositions, 36-37, 41, 44, 54-56, 78, 92, 134
Correspondence courses, 122
Cosmetics, 69
Costume, 72-74, 103

Demonstrations, step-by-step, see procedures
Drawing, 37-39, 53-63, 78, 87-90, 97, 123; see also Features, Observing, Sketching

Ears, 55, 69-72; illus. of, 56, 70-71
Earth colors, 108
Easels, 21; types of, 32-33; illus. of, 32
Education, 19, 89-90, 117-123, 124-138 *passim.;* see also Drawing, Observing, Sketching

Equipment, 54, 89, 115; lists of basic, 21-23; see also Canvas, Colors, Easels, Mediums, etc.
Exhibiting, 15, 138
Eyes, 60, 63, 69, 80, 81, 134; illus. of, 64-65
Eyebrow, placement of, 55

Farnsworth, Jerry, illus. by, 2, 10, 13, 14, 16, 18, 20, 22, 26, 40, 44-51, 52, 58, 68, 75, 76, 78-85, 86, 91-96, 98, 101, 106, 113, 116, 121, 124, 126, 128, 134, 139
Features, proportions of, 54-56, 60, 72; illus. of, 55, 56, 64-65, 66-67, 70-71; see also Ears, Eyes, Mouth, etc.
Fixative, 21; use of, 39; see also Medium
Fugitive colors, 24

Gluckmann, Grigory, illus. by, 119

Hair, 79, 81, 92
Half-light, 57, 59-60; illus. of, 61; see also Shadows
Hands, 54, 72; size of, illus. of, 55
Hansen, Ejnar, illus. by, 104
Harmony, 37, 131
Hawthorne, Charles W., 36
Head, 54, 136; illus. of, 55, 56
Henri, Robert, 133
Highlights, 63, 72, 133; see also Light

Impasto, see Scraping

Kerosene, 31-32
Knives, see Palette knife
Koch, John, illus. by, 109
Kroll, Leon, illus. by, 130

Landscapes, 122
Light, see Half-light, Highlights, Reflected light, Shadows
Linseed oil, 27, 115

Mars colors, 25, 108
Materials, see Equipment
Masonite, 29
McFee, Henry Lee, illus. by, 38
Medium, 27, 43, 115, 131
Mixing, see Colors
Mineral spirits, 32
Modeling, see Features, Highlights, Shadows, Skin
Moses, Grandma, 15
Mouth, 69, 81; illus. of, 66-67
Muscles, 60; see also Anatomy

Nose, 55, 60

Nudes, painting of, 87-90; illus. of, 62, 86, 88, 91-96, 106, 109, 116, 124, 126, 130

Observing, importance of, 11-12, 35-36, 39, 41, 89-90; see also Drawing, Sketching

Palette, 24-25; illus. of, arrangement of, 25
Palette knife: types of 21, illus. of, 30; use of, 30, 41; illus. of, 46-51
Pastel colors, 131
Permanent colors, see Colors
Personality: painter's, 132; sitter's, 100-103
Philipp, Robert, illus. by, 88
Posing, 57, 89, 91, 134; see also Shadows
Pricing, 105, 120
Procedures, step-by-step: nude, illus. of, 91-96; portrait, 53-63, illus. of, 78-85; still life, 41, illus. of, 44-51; see also Drawing, Sketching
Profiles, 55-59; illus. of, 55, 56, 61; lost, 53, 57-59, 94, 134; illus. of, 58
Proportions, see Composition, Features

Reflected light, 59-60; illus. of, 61
Retouching, 32, 43, 77

Saint-Gaudens, Homer, 12-14
Scraping, 32, 77, 129
Scumbling, 31; see also Brushes
Shadows, 41, 56, 60; illus. of, 61, 79, 82, 83, 84, 89; see also Light
Shellac, 29
Silhouette, 60, 63
Sizing, 28-29; see also Canvas
Sketching, 39; see also Drawing, Observing
Skin, 60-63, 72, 80
Skull, see Head
Speicher, Eugene, 107; illus. by, 73
Stretchers, 21, 28-29; see also Canvas
Still life, 36-51
Subjects, see Observing
Sunday painting, 15; see also Careers, Education

Talent, development of, 11-19, 117-123, 125-136 *passim*.
Taste, 11-15, 99-100
"Tooth," see Canvas
Turpentine, 27, 29, 78, 115; see also Medium

Varnish, 27, 43, 77, 115; see also Medium

White, use of, 129; see also Colors, White lead, Zinc white
White lead, use of, 28, 111-114, 115
Wyeth, Andrew, 118-120

Zinc white, use of, 111-114